Education for Public Democracy

SUNY Series, Teacher Empowerment and School Reform
Edited by Henry A. Giroux and Peter L. McLaren

SUNY Series, Democracy and Education
Edited by George H. Wood

Education for Public Democracy

David T. Sehr

STATE UNIVERSITY OF NEW YORK PRESS

Published by
State University of New York Press, Albany

For information, address State University of New York Press,
State University Plaza, Albany, N.Y., 12246

Production by Cathleen Collins
Marketing by Nancy Farrell

Library of Congress Cataloging in Publication Data

Sehr, David T., 1958–
     Education for public democracy / David T. Sehr.
         p. cm. — (SUNY series, teacher empowerment and school
     reform) (SUNY series, democracy and education)
     Includes bibliographical references and index.
     ISBN 0-7914-3167-3 (alk. paper). — ISBN 0-7914-3168-1 (pbk. :
     alk. paper)
     1. Critical pedagogy—United States.   2. Education—United States—
     Philosophy—History.   3. Democracy—Study and teaching (Secondary)—
     United States.   I. Title.   II. Series.   III. Series: Teacher
     empowerment and school reform.
     LC196.5.U6S45 1997
     370.11'5'0973—dc20   96-1079
                                                              CIP

10 9 8 7 6 5 4 3 2 1

To Maria, my partner in life and my inspiration as a democratic teacher.

And to Matthew Martin, our son, whose prospects for living in a more equitable, just, and democratic society will depend, in part, on the transformation of American education.

Contents

Acknowledgments ix

Introduction 1

Part I. American Democracy: Privatized or Public? 9

1. Democratic Ideology, Hegemony and Education 11

2. Ideological Roots of Privatized and Public Democracy:
   Contrasting Locke and the Federalists with Rousseau
   and Jefferson 31

3. Privatized Democracy: Nineteenth- and
   Twentieth-Century Ideology and Practice 43

4. Public Democracy 57

5. Education for Public Democratic Citizenship 83

Part II. Democratic Education? Tales from Two Schools 107

6. Structure and Organization of Two Democratic
   High Schools 111

7. Curriculum and Pedagogy in Two Democratic
   High Schools 129

8. Promoting Public Democratic Citizenship: Student
   Responses to School Programs   145

9. In Search of Public Democratic Education   171

   Bibliography   181

   Index   191

Acknowledgments

Many people have supported, encouraged, and helped me in numerous concrete ways as I have completed the research and writing of this book.

I must first thank Stanley Aronowitz, whose understanding and shared belief in the value of this project helped nurture my earliest ideas, and their development into this completed work.

I am also grateful for insightful responses to various drafts of the book by Ann Cook, Richard Gibboney, and Stan Karp. Their comments helped me correct factual errors, reduce the use of academic jargon, and write a book which remains theoretically informed, yet is also grounded in the practical realities and struggles of democratic high school teachers and their students.

I must also thank the teachers, students, and administrators of the real and inspiring schools which lie behind the pseudonyms of Uptown High School and Metropolitan High School. They graciously welcomed me into their classrooms, corridors, and offices, and shared with me their visions of democratic high school education. These educators are doing this country's most important work. They are recreating the institution of education, finding new ways to awaken young minds, in the hope that their students will help awaken our democracy.

Finally, I want to thank my wife, Maria Sweeney, for all she has done to support me in this project. She has assisted me in every possible way, reading chapter drafts, suggesting additional resources I should consult, and helping me sharpen my writing and my thinking. She has also accepted additional burdens of home and family life, while maintaining her own demanding professional life, to give me the opportunity to write. She has put up with this book as a constant house guest, a kind of interesting but burdensome in-law who moved into our house several years ago, and is only now making tentative plans to move out. Throughout this project's "visit" with us, Maria has maintained her faith in me, supporting me in my writing and my career moves, as we have started our family together. Nothing I say here can even begin to express how important her support has been. I can only say that she has been the perfect partner in this work, as she is in every aspect of our life together.

Introduction

Behind the current clamor for educational reform, restructuring, privatization, and vouchers, is the assumption that the purpose of public education is to prepare Americans to compete, both as individuals and as a society, in the new global economic order. With better education, the thinking goes, individuals will qualify for better, higher-paying jobs. With a better-educated workforce, American society as a whole will prosper.

There is a tragic irony here. As deindustrialization, automation and downsizing have become the permanent watchwords of the American economy, the connection between education and job opportunities has become increasingly tenuous.[1] A generation of young Americans is growing up with the nagging (and accurate) suspicion, that regardless of their educational achievements, there simply aren't many good jobs for them.

As Americans nevertheless accept as common sense the notion that the purpose of education is a strictly economic one, we lose sight of public education's original and fundamental purpose. When Thomas Jefferson first proposed public education in his state of Virginia, his intent was to expand the participation of an educated

---

1. Stanley Aronowitz, "A Different Perspective on Educational Inequality," in *Experiencing Diversity: Toward Educational Equity*, ed. Frank Pignatelli and Susanna W. Pflaum (Thousand Oaks, CA: Corwin Press, 1994), 36–38.

public in preserving and strengthening *democracy*.[2] Now more than ever, Americans need to reinvigorate the traditional, fundamentally political and democratic purposes of education espoused by Jefferson, John Dewey and other democratic educational thinkers. American educators need to reaffirm their commitment to "the purpose of helping students become more active participants in the civic life of their neighborhoods, their cities, and the larger world."[3]

Even a casual glance at the news makes it clear that American society, and the democracy that should be at its heart, are facing severe challenges. This country's mounting social ills can only be addressed through the active efforts of citizens to expand their power, vitalize their democracy and take greater control over their government and their lives. Public education must help prepare young people to take up this challenge.

In recent years, a number of writers have called for "democratic education," or "critical" or "empowering education."[4] These theorists have moved beyond standard critiques of education's links to the economy and to reproduction of unequal race and class relations. They have begun to create a "language of possibility" with which to imagine more democratic forms of education.[5] To carry this project forward, it is necessary to begin to connect more directly the language of possibility in theory with a new language of possibility in democratic educational practice. In this way, those who wish to develop democratic educational practices will be able to learn from the experience of others who are working toward this goal. As Jesse Goodman puts it:

> What is needed is to build upon the language of possibility by developing an educational language of democratic imagery, that

---

2. Thomas Jefferson, *Notes on the State of Virginia*, ed. William Peden (New York: W. W. Norton, 1982, orig., 1787), 148–149).

3. Aronowitz, 1994, 41.

4. To name just a few: M. Apple, *Ideology and Curriculum* (New York: Routledge and Kegan Paul, 1979); S. Aronowitz and H. Giroux, *Education under Siege* (London: Routledge & Kegan Paul, 1985) and *Postmodern Education* (Minneapolis: University of Minnesota Press, 1991); Giroux, *Schooling and the Struggle for Public Life*; J. Goodman, *Elementary Schooling for Critical Democracy* (Albany: SUNY Press, 1992); Peter McLaren, *Life in Schools* (New York: Longman, 1989); I. Shor, *Critical Teaching and Everyday Life* (Boston: South End Press, 1980) and *Empowering Education* (Chicago: University of Chicago Press, 1992); K. Weiler, *Women Teaching for Change* (South Hadley, MA: Bergin and Garvey, 1988.

5. Aronowitz and Giroux, *Education under Siege*, 154.

is, a theoretical language which is informed by and rooted in images of real . . . people involved in tangible actions that take place in actual settings.[6]

We need research that explores and analyzes the curriculum and teaching practices, as well as the lived experiences of students and teachers, in existing schools which are trying to provide democratic education. Qualitative research, based on extensive observation and interviews, can offer detailed and complex insights into the workings of such schools. However, when researchers and educators look at a school, it is not enough to interpret their findings strictly in terms of the socially constructed cultures within that particular school. For researchers to interpret their findings in this limited way is to disassociate what goes on in schools from the larger culture and society.[7]

Instead, researchers and educators working to create democratic education must begin by asking themselves a simple, yet profound question: What do we mean by democracy and democratic citizenship? Most democratic educational theorists, researchers and educators fail to consider this question. Or if they consider it, they fail to articulate a clear, detailed vision of the personal qualities and abilities an individual would need to be an active, effective citizen in a democratic society. Such a vision is necessary for researchers and educators who wish to analyze systematically the curricula and teaching practices in schools which aspire to promote democratic citizenship. Only if we have a clear vision of the qualities necessary for effective democratic citizenship, can we assess the degree to which a "democratic" school promotes those qualities in young people.

The chief task of part I of this book is to consider in some depth the question of what we as Americans mean by democracy and citizenship. In formulating a vision of effective democratic citizenship, it quickly becomes apparent that there are, in fact, competing

---

6. Goodman, 173.

7. An example of this phenomenon: Jesse Goodman notes that Alan Peshkin's otherwise insightful ethnography of a fundamentalist Christian school, fails to make an important connection between what goes on in the school and the larger social and ideological context. The "study fails to illuminate the way in which the teachings of this school reflect the secular, conservative ideology that dominates our society, which in turn keeps current relations of power and privilege intact." See Goodman, 36, on A. Peshkin, *God's Choice: The Total World of a Fundamentalist Christian School* (Chicago: Chicago University Press, 1986).

understandings of what democracy and citizenship should be in the United States. Although there are perhaps as many differing conceptions of citizenship as there are democratic theorists, there are two major ideological strains that have vied to define American democratic thinking and practice since the country's founding.

The first, dominant ideological tradition, *privatized democracy*, is rooted in the political thought of Hobbes and Locke, and the authors of *The Federalist Papers*, Madison, Hamilton, and Jay. Other shapers of this tradition were the nineteenth-century utilitarian liberals, and twentieth-century American pluralist theorists and free-market economists. This conception of democracy minimizes the role of ordinary citizens as political actors who can shape their collective destiny through participation with others in public life. Instead, it reinforces an egoistic individualism, and a glorification of materialism and consumerism as the keys to personal happiness and fulfillment. Its faith in the powers of a "free market" of self-serving individuals, guided by an invisible hand of Providence, in the political as well as the economic realms, denies the possibility of conscious, collective efforts to serve a public good. It denies, in principal, that people can come together to govern themselves. This dominant ideology has produced a profound weakness at the heart of contemporary American democracy and social life.

As this book argues in chapter 1, Americans' experience of the dominant ideology and practice of privatized democracy limits possibilities for changing and reinvigorating American democracy. Privatized democracy maintains itself through the constant reinforcement of people's experience of "commonsense" notions and everyday practices of democracy. This process of system maintenance is known as hegemony. As a result of the hegemony of privatized democracy, most Americans can barely even imagine participating in public life to serve a common good. And if they could imagine it, most would lack the tools to do so.

However, as chapter 1 also explains, the dominance of privatized democracy has been challenged historically by a second, alternative ideology and practice of democracy, *public democracy*. Public democracy is grounded in the work of Rousseau and Jefferson, with more recent theoretical contributions coming from Dewey, Mills, and a number of important feminist writers.

Public democracy sees people's participation in public life as the essential ingredient in democratic government. Public participation arises out of an ethic of care and responsibility, not only for oneself as an isolated individual, but for one's fellow citizens as co-builders and co-beneficiaries of the public good. Public democratic ideas and practices can revitalize American democracy and renew American society.

It is important for researchers and educators interested in democratic schooling to comprehend this larger context of competing understandings and practices of democracy in the United States. Progressive educators can draw ideological clarity, strength and legitimacy from the alternative, public democratic tradition, as they seek to prepare young people to participate in expanding American democracy.

Chapter 2 explores the early ideological roots of privatized and public democracy. It focuses particularly on the ideas of Locke and Madison on the one hand, and Rousseau and Jefferson on the other. Chapter 3 examines nineteenth– and twentieth–century democratic and economic ideology, as well as political participation patterns which have supported the dominance of privatized democracy in the United States. Chapter 4 draws on Dewey, C. Wright Mills, Nancy Fraser, Carol Gilligan, Carol Gould, and other feminist thinkers to construct an alternative vision of American democracy. The chapter culminates in a discussion of a number of ideal characteristics that a person should possess to be able to function as a public democratic citizen. Chapter 5 takes the ideal public citizenship characteristics as a guide for sketching the outlines of a secondary school that would promote these qualities in young people. This ideal image is proposed as a tool for examining the organization and practices of existing schools that seek to provide public democratic education.

Part II of the book explores the possibilities for creating education for public democratic citizenship, within an urban public high school context. It applies the analytical tool developed in part I to sample analyses of the organizational features and educational practices of two existing urban alternative public high schools. Chapters 6 and 7 offer an overview of the structure, organization, curricula, and teaching approaches in the two high schools. These aspects of the two schools are analyzed in terms of their effectiveness in engaging students in activities that promote public democratic citizenship qualities. Chapter 8 examines two exemplary classes, one in each high school. Examination of these two classes leads to important insights about how students respond to the organization and educational practices of the two schools. The final chapter draws some conclusions about the importance of public democratic education, and the complexities of actually attempting to create it in urban public high schools.

This book is ambitious in that it attempts to present a solid theoretical foundation for understanding some of the contradictions of American democracy. Then, based on that theoretical understanding, it creates a tool for analyzing schools that hope to prepare young people for public democracy. Finally, it uses its theoretically based analytical tool to examine the workings of two existing alternative public high schools.

Because of this broad scope, different readers may want to read the book in different ways to satisfy their various purposes and interests. Academics and other educators interested in the place of public democratic education in the complex process of ideological, social and political change in the United States will want to read this book in the order in which it is written. This will establish a clear theoretical foundation for the categories of analysis used to examine the schools in part II.

Teachers, school administrators and others who are oriented more toward school practice, may want to begin with part II. This will get them immediately into a description and analysis of the two schools that were studied. They may refer back to tables 4.1 on page 79, 5.1 on page 87, and 5.2 on page 89 in part I as needed, to get a sketch of what is meant by public democratic citizenship and public democratic education, and to clarify the categories of analysis that are used to examine the two schools. After reading part II, it would be important to return to a more detailed reading of part I, focusing especially on chapters 4 and 5. This approach allows readers to see sample analyses of important aspects of the schools in action, before going back to consider the theoretical foundations of public democratic citizenship and education for public democracy.

Educators working for public democracy have a dual task before them. First, they must understand clearly what public democratic citizenship entails, and what kinds of school structures and practices promote it. Then, they must examine their existing schools, or their plans for new schools, through the lens of public democracy. This book seeks to clarify what public democratic citizenship is, and develop a lens democratic educators can use in their work recreating American education.

PART I

American Democracy: Privatized or Public?

CHAPTER 1

Democratic Ideology, Hegemony and Education

The State of American Democracy and Democratic Consciousness

Since the birth of the U.S. republic, dominant strains of American political thinking and institutional practice have worked to limit and erode the idea of active participation by ordinary people in the project of self-government. The impulse to contain the presumed evils of participatory democracy is built into the foundation of American government, the Constitution. It is explained and defended in the famous essays of the *Federalist Papers*.

This political tradition has to its credit some undeniable contributions to democracy, in particular the protection of essential individual rights and freedoms. In a world where religious fanaticism, political repression, ethnic cleansing, and other affronts to individuals and groups are too often official government policies, the protection of individual rights and freedoms is no small accomplishment. However, the limited-participation, individualistic vision that has dominated American democracy has proven unable to cope with the serious social problems that have accompanied late-twentieth-century American capitalism.

Now even the limited participatory aspects of American liberal representative government are falling into decay. Americans' faith in government, and their interest in public affairs have hit bottom.

11

Alienation has become a central indicator of modern political crisis [in the U.S.], whether it is measured by plummeting electoral participation figures, widespread distrust of politicians, or pervasive apathy about things public and political.[1]

This is especially true of young people. As Michael Oreskes of the *New York Times* puts it,

While apathy and alienation have become a national plague, the disengagement seems to run deeper among young Americans, those 18 to 29, setting them clearly apart from earlier generations.[2]

Oreskes cites two separate reports to support this claim. First, a report by the Times Mirror Center for the People and the Press states that this generation of young citizens "knows less, cares less, votes less and is less critical of its leaders and institutions than young people in the past." A second report, by People for the American Way, argues that there is a "citizenship crisis" and that "America's youth are alarmingly ill-prepared to keep democracy alive in the 1990s and beyond."[3]

Young Americans appreciate their presumed freedom to do what they want. When their actions or speech are questioned they are often quick with the cliched defense, "This is a free country, isn't it?" But they "fail to grasp the other half of the democratic equation: the responsibility to participate in the hard work of self-

---

1. Benjamin Barber, *Strong Democracy* (Los Angeles: University of California Press, 1984), xiii.

Although voter participation in the 1992 presidential election (55% of the voting age population) was the highest since 1972, this was likely an anomaly, due to the appeal of third-party candidate Ross Perot among alienated voters who had not voted in recent years (Robert Pear, "55% Voting Rate Reverses 30-Year Decline," *New York Times*, 5 November 1992). The voter participation rate in the midterm congressional elections of 1994, despite all the hoopla about the Contract with America, was only 44.6%—lower than the rates in the last two midterm elections (45% in 1990 and 46% in 1986) ("Low-Income Voters' Turnout Fell in 1994, Census Reports," *New York Times*, 11 June 1995, p. 28). As is well known, both these participation figures are embarrassingly low in comparison with voter participation rates in most other Western democracies.

2. Michael Oreskes, "A Trait of Today's Youth: Apathy to Public Affairs," *The New York Times*, 28 June 1990, A1.

3. Ibid.

government."[4] They show little interest in government, politics, current events or public life.[5]

Among Americans, and especially young Americans, there is a widespread sense of political alienation and a mass rejection of the idea of participation in public life. The only times many Americans get involved in public debate, or even vote, is when a major political scandal surfaces, or when they perceive the threat of a war, a tax increase, or some other problem that might directly affect their personal lives. Alienation from public life leads to a diminished sense of citizenship as merely flag-waving, artificial patriotism. Such citizens pledge their allegiance to the flag, and then stand by as their government and corporate leaders go about their business, with or without regard for liberty and justice.[6]

Current Directions in American Social Life

If American citizens remain withdrawn from public life, our society will continue to be shaped, by default, by members of the following two groups: (1) the richest, most powerful, and influential business and finance leaders, who help shape the economy in which most people earn their living and seek satisfaction of their consumer needs and wants; and (2) those who do participate regularly and powerfully in public life and government. This second group includes both issue-oriented interest groups[7] and, again, powerful business and finance leaders, who because of their economic importance can exercise their influence through both formal and informal means. In many cases the members of these two groups represent the same or similar social class interests—those of business and the upper classes.[8]

---

4. People for the American Way, *Democracy's Next Generation: A Study of Youth and Teachers* (People for the American Way, 1989), 14–15.

5. Ibid., 16, 30–31.

6. Walter Karp finds this false, antidemocratic patriotism, which he calls "nationism," to be rampant in late-twentieth century American society. Walter Karp, "The Two Americas," in *Buried Alive: Essays on Our Endangered Republic* (New York: Franklin Square Press, 1992), 13–26.

7. There are many of these groups, but some of the obvious ones are the National Rifle Association, anti-gun groups, anti-abortion groups, abortion rights groups, the Christian Coalition, etc.

8. E. E. Schattschneider, *The Semisovereign People: A Realist's View of Democracy in America* (Hinsdale, IL: Dryden Press, 1975, orig., 1966), 20–45.

As people have become increasingly alienated from public life, those left as stewards of American society have established a record of their achievements. If this record portends future developments, most Americans have reason for concern. Below are just a few indicators of the disastrous direction in which our political guardians are taking us, as many Americans remain politically disengaged.

Enormous Concentration of Wealth

- "The share of net worth . . . held by the top 1 percent of households jumped from below 20 percent in 1979 to more than 36 percent in 1989." The number of American billionaires leaped from 21 in 1982 to 71 in 1991. "The wealthy's share of the total wealth expanded as much during the Reagan boom as it did in the 100 years—roughly 1830 to 1929—in which America transformed itself from an egalitarian land of small farmers into the world's reigning industrial power."[9]
- During the 1980s, the income of the richest Americans (those in the top 20% of the nation in family income) increased their share of national family income from 46.7% to 51.4%.[10]
- While corporate presidents' earnings "soared to 160 times that of the average worker, union membership sank, and pay and productivity . . . stagnated."[11]

Shrinking Middle Class; Growing Lower Class

- Between 1972 and 1988, real weekly pay of both white collar and blue collar workers fell by 11% in constant dollars.[12]
- Between 1969 and 1989, the percentage of Americans with middle incomes fell from 71.2% to 63.3%. During the same

9. Sylvia Nasar, "The Rich Get Richer, But Never the Same Way Twice," *The New York Times*, 16 August 1992, section 4, 3.

10. Kevin Phillips, *Boiling Point: Democrats, Republicans and the Decline of Middle-Class Prosperity* (New York: Harper Collins, 1994), 279.

11. Nasar, 3.

12. Kevin Phillips, *The Politics of Rich and Poor* (New York: Random House, 1990), 18.

period, the percentage of Americans with low incomes (less than half the median income) rose from 17.9% to 22.1%.[13]

- Since 1979, "the percentage of all Americans working full time but earning less than the poverty level for a family of four, about $13,000 a year, has risen by 50 percent."[14]
- The percentage of young workers (age 18–24) earning less than the poverty level has more than doubled, from 23 percent in 1979 to 47 percent in 1992.[15]

Tax Burden Shifted Downward

- During the 1980s the top federal tax bracket was cut from 70% to 30%.[16]
- Between 1960 and 1986, the effective tax rate on corporate profits was cut from 46% to 21%.[17]
- As a result of the 1986 federal tax reform, families earning a million dollars a year or more received a 31% tax cut, saving them over $280,000 per year. People earning $30,000–$40,000 got only an 11% tax cut, giving them about $467 a year in additional take-home pay.[18]

Homes and Homelessness

- "The U.S. leads the 19 major industrial nations in homelessness and in percentage of people living in big homes [5 rooms or more]."[19]

---

13. U.S. Census Bureau report, cited in "Middle Class Shrinks, U.S. Says," *The New York Times*, 22 February 1992, I, 9.

14. Jason DeParle, "Sharp Increase Along the Borders of Poverty," *The New York Times*, 31 March 1994.

15. Ibid.

16. Sylvia Nasar, "The Rich Get Richer..."

17. Steve Brouwer, *Sharing the Pie: A Disturbing Picture of the U.S. Economy* (Carlisle, PA: Big Picture Books, 1992), 9.

18. Phillips, 1994, figure 4, 113.

19. Andrew L. Shapiro, *We're Number One!* (New York: Vintage Books, 1992), 77.

- Homelessness in the U.S. doubled between 1983 and 1987, and by 1992, the U.S. Coalition for the Homeless put the number of homeless Americans at three million.[20] A 1994 report by Andrew Cuomo of the U.S. Department of Housing and Urban Development "argues that seven million people were homeless at some point during the latter half of the 1980s."[21]

Prisons and Schools

- The U.S. has the highest rate of incarceration in the world, jailing 426 of every 100,000 people. The U.S. prison population has more than doubled since 1979.[22]
- The U.S. ranks seventeenth in the world in public spending on education per Gross Domestic Product.[23] Federal spending on education fell 18% between 1979 and 1991.[24]

These and similar trends have been especially severe in America's cities. Cities have become plagued with the sharp contradictions of extreme wealth and poverty; flight of manufacturing jobs which pay a middle-class wage; burgeoning homelessness; cutbacks in federal expenditures for urban services and programs for the poor; continued de facto school segregation between city and suburb; the destruction of communities by violence and drugs; the lack of economic opportunity for minimally skilled people, and especially people of color; worsening patterns of racial and gender bias and discrimination; rising tension between the police and communities of people of color; and continual fiscal austerity, limiting the possibilities for public policy responses to these problems.

The quality of life of the majority of Americans has deteriorated dramatically in recent years. The foundation for our collective future as a society is cracking. The 1992 street uprising in Los Angeles following the acquittals of police officers who had been videotaped

---

20. Ibid., 78.
21. Kevin Sack, "Andrew Cuomo," *The New York Times Magazine* 27 March 1994, 42.
22. Tom Wicker, "The Iron Medal," *The New York Times*, 7 January 1991.
23. Shapiro, 56.
24. Brouwer, 21.

beating Rodney King, is both a symptom of this deterioration and a warning. As Cornel West sees it, "What we witnessed in Los Angeles was the consequence of a lethal linkage of economic decline, cultural decay and political lethargy in American life."[25]

The Need for Public Democracy

If the United States is to address its mounting social problems, there will have to be much broader and fuller participation in the decision-making processes that shape society. People must reenter— or in many cases enter for the first time—the public life of their society. Privately oriented individuals must become active, effective, publicly oriented citizens. They must organize to take control of the powerful institutions of society, or create new social institutions through which to build social justice, fairness, equality, economic opportunity—in short, the conditions necessary for the self-development of all members of society.[26] Democracy must be revived and widely expanded to ensure that society's broadest possible interests will be served.

However, social change as fundamental as the invigoration of American democracy cannot take place in the present political and ideological climate. A challenge must first be mounted to the existing system of hegemony, that is, to the system of ideas and social practices that helps maintain the domination of corporate and upper-class interests over those of the rest of the population.[27] In the United States, this domination is maintained, in part, by a system of ideas and practices that promotes large-scale alienation and disengagement from public life.

Current dominant *conceptions* of democracy and of a citizen's role in a democracy, following a long tradition in liberal political

---

25. Cornel West, "Learning to Talk of Race," *The New York Times Magazine*, 2 August 1992, 24.

26. Carol Gould, *Rethinking Democracy: Freedom and Social Cooperation in Politics, Economy and Society* (New York: Cambridge University Press, 1988), 110.

27. Antonio Gramsci, one of the earliest, most important theorists of hegemony, defines social hegemony as the " 'spontaneous' consent given by the great masses of the population to the general direction imposed on social life" by the dominant class. See Antonio Gramsci, *Selections from the Prison Notebooks*, ed. and transl. Quintin Hoare and Geoffrey Nowell Smith (New York: International Publishers, 1985), 12.

and social thought, are only minimally concerned with participation in public life. They are oriented chiefly toward individual, private economic activity as the fulfillment of the promise of democracy. The *traditional practice* of democracy in the United States has also been one of limited participation by most people in government and public affairs. This combination of dominant American ideas and traditional practices of democracy, has contributed to what can be called an American hegemonic ideology of democracy that favors low levels of popular democratic participation and a withering of the public sphere.

American society is deteriorating precisely because most people are not participating purposefully and powerfully in public life, either as individuals or as members of organized groups. Most Americans have neither the experience (democratic practice) nor the inclination (ideological impetus) to participate in shaping their society. Nor do they have the necessary knowledge and skills for effective democratic participation. If the United States wishes to halt its current slide toward social decay and begin to build a just, inclusive, prosperous, and democratic future, the current hegemonic ideology of democracy will have to be challenged. It will need to be replaced by an alternative ideology and related practice of *public democracy*.

Hegemony and the Role of Intellectuals in Social Stability and Social Change

Hegemony is an ongoing process, "a complex interlocking of political, social and cultural forces," that supports a particular social order.[28] Hegemony is maintained through all of society's cultural and social processes, as they interact with, and enter into the practical consciousness of individuals.[29]

---

28. Raymond Williams, *Marxism and Literature* (New York: Oxford University Press, 1977), 108. There are many interpretations of Gramsci's ideas on hegemony. In this book, the terms "hegemony" and "hegemonic ideologies" will be used in the sense laid out by Raymond Williams. That is, the terms will not be used to mean merely dominant sets of ideas or explanations of the world, but will also include the sense of concrete everyday practices that are connected with such ideas, in a mutually reinforcing, dialectical relationship.

29. Ibid., 110.

The process of hegemony creates for most people a "sense of reality" that attempts to place beyond question or criticism much of social life, including the existing relations of domination and subordination within which different social groups live.[30] Through the process of hegemony, people come to see unequal power relations in society as merely "the pressures and limits of simple experience and common sense."[31] Injustice and inequality are taken for granted as natural, commonsense realities.

Nevertheless, because hegemony is a living social process, it carries within it seeds of change. As Raymond Williams describes it:

> A lived hegemony . . . is a realized complex of experiences, relationships and activities, with specific and changing pressures and limits. . . . It has continually to be renewed, recreated, defended, and modified. It is also continually resisted, limited, altered, challenged by pressures not at all its own. We have then to add to the concept of hegemony the concepts of counter-hegemony and alternative hegemony . . .
>
> The reality of any hegemony . . . is that, while by definition it is always dominant, it is never either total or exclusive. At any time, forms of alternative or directly oppositional politics and culture exist as significant elements in the society.[32]

In order to understand how a hegemonic ideology of democracy in the United States might be challenged, it is necessary to examine the role of intellectuals in establishing and maintaining hegemony. As has been said, hegemony is a complex social process that results in the manufacture and reinforcement of public consent to the existing social order. Intellectuals play a central role in this process.[33] They take key positions in civil society and government, and serve the dominant classes through their work in the institutions of business, education, religion, communications, culture, politics, and so on.[34] They direct and manage the organizational and technical work

---

30. Ibid.
31. Ibid.
32. Ibid., 112–13.
33. The term "intellectuals" is used here in a broad sense, referring not only to academics, but also to whole strata of technically skilled and educated people, from artists to corporate leaders to politicians.
34. Gramsci, 12.

of business. Intellectuals perform similar functions in the bureaucratic and political work of government. They also fill directive and technical positions in the law enforcement, justice, and penal systems, as well in the military. Through these roles, intellectuals help shape the everyday practices of the vast majority of individuals. In addition, intellectuals take active roles in ideological production as teachers, writers, artists, philosophers, scientists, religious functionaries, news and other media figures, entertainers, and so on.

If intellectuals fail to play their roles in the construction and management of social hegemony, or if they play counterhegemonic roles, mass consent to a social order can begin to erode. If this occurs, dominant groups must attempt to reestablish public consent to the social order. If the erosion of public consent becomes very deep, it can sometimes only be reestablished around somewhat altered social relations and practices. When this happens, social change occurs.

In order to challenge the dominance of privatized democracy in the United States, there is a need for intellectuals who will serve the cause of expanding democracy. These intellectuals will be needed as spokespeople and leaders of social movements that challenge privatized democracy with new visions of public democracy. In fact, full participation in public democracy will require the development of *all* members of society as intellectuals, so that all are capable of engaging in public life, and when necessary, taking up roles as leaders for social change. Antonio Gramsci's understanding of intellectuals supports this egalitarian vision of a democratic society in which all citizens are intellectually prepared to participate in public life.

Two Types of Intellectuals

Gramsci identifies two main types of intellectuals—*organic intellectuals* and *traditional intellectuals*. Both types play important roles in determining whether a social order will be maintained or whether an existing hegemony will be challenged.

Traditional intellectuals are intellectuals whose positions in society were established under previously existing social relations of production. They have remained in existence despite far-reaching social transformations. Examples of traditional intellectuals are ecclesiastics, such as theologians, clergy and religious administrators, religious teachers, and charity workers; and secular intellectuals such as philosophers, academics, scientists, and artists.[35] Traditional intellectuals tend to see themselves as an autonomous, independent social group, unbeholden to other social classes as they pursue physical or metaphysical "truths." To a limited extent they are correct. Some intellectuals still feel more closely allied to their own traditional institutions and historical practices than they do to the institutions and causes of current social classes and groups—whether dominant or subordinate. However, these intellectuals find themselves drawn increasingly toward enlistment in the positions and causes of newer social classes and groups. Traditional intellectuals become targeted for recruitment to the causes of both dominant and subordinate social groups.

An example of this phenomenon is provided by the traditional intellectuals of the Catholic Church. The Catholic clergy are ostensibly loyal to the Church's stated primary mission of saving souls and helping people live a more spiritual life. This is certainly the way the Pope and the Church hierarchy in Rome would have it. Historically, however, the Church has usually aligned itself with the existing social order in any given country, and its intellectuals have supported that social order through their organizational and ideological work. Even when the Church's intellectuals have focused almost exclusively on spiritual life, this has had the effect, by default, of supporting existing material social relations.

But through the theology of liberation, Catholic clergy and lay intellectuals in Latin America and other parts of the world have become embroiled in a quite worldly class struggle. Many have chosen a "preferential option for the poor," and now organize and work on the side of the poor for greater social justice and more equitable social relations. Others have continued to support the existing social order. But in countries like El Salvador and Brazil, where social inequality and injustice are stark, and where the forces for and against fundamental social change have become so hotly engaged, there has been little room for Church people to remain outside the struggle. In recent visits to Latin America, the

---

35. Ibid., 7.

Pope himself has felt compelled to call publicly for greater social justice and equality, even though he strongly rejects liberation theology, and has done much to attempt to neutralize its clergy practitioners.[36]

A similar case can be made about traditional, secular intellectuals. They often present themselves as autonomous, non-class-aligned individuals, busily pursuing their truths in the arts, sciences or other academic fields. Yet the social base that provides for the independence and 'intellectual freedom' of these intellectuals is relatively narrow and weak. Take, for example, the university. The university is perhaps the single most important institutional base for these intellectuals, yet this is clearly a site that is highly influenced by the dominant classes. Universities receive significant portions of their operating monies from corporate grants and contracts, which tie scientists, artists, and other intellectuals into projects that directly and indirectly serve corporate interests. Universities are even more dependent on the state. To the extent that the state acts in the service of the dominant classes, universities and their intellectuals are further brought into the service of the dominant classes.

However, as Louis Althusser points out, universities, as ideological state apparatuses, are sites of ideological struggle.[37] Some traditional intellectuals in universities will no doubt be recruited to work for the dominant classes. Some will attempt to maintain an independent stance, serving as well as they can the ideals of their intellectual and institutional traditions. Nevertheless, what these independently oriented traditional intellectuals create—lectures, research papers, articles, books—are cultural products, which as such will become the object of ideological contestation. Both dominant and insurgent social groups will attempt to use these cultural products (when they deal with relevant social issues), to support their hegemonic or alternative hegemonic positions. Other traditional intellectuals will work directly in the service of insurgent subordinate social groups. Through their research and organizational work they

36. Alan Cowell, "Pope Challenges Brazil Leaders on Behalf of Poor," *New York Times*, 15 October 1991, A–15.

37. Louis Althusser, "Ideology and Ideological State Apparatuses (Notes Towards an Investigation)," in *Lenin and Philosophy and Other Essays* (New York: Monthly Review Press, 1971), 127–86.

will support the causes of the poor, people of color, feminists, environmentalists, and others who challenge the injustices of the existing social order. So traditional intellectuals are indeed a group that is open for recruitment to the causes of both dominant and subordinate social groups.

Organic intellectuals arise in connection with the emergence of new social classes. Unlike traditional intellectuals, who see themselves as independent of class interests, organic intellectuals perform essential economic, social, and political functions for the classes with which they are connected. The capitalist class, for example, develops its own (or recruits from other classes) managers, technicians, lawyers, politicians, academics, and cultural agents such as artists and writers. These groups organize and maintain the unequal social relations of capitalism through their work in business, government, and cultural production.[38]

Subordinate social groups, especially those that are rising to challenge the inequalities and injustices of the existing social order, can also develop or recruit their own organic intellectuals. These are the people who, regardless of what jobs or professions they have, serve their social classes or groups as leaders and organizers. Such leaders as Cesar Chavez and Martin Luther King, Jr. were prominent examples of organic intellectuals of subordinate groups. But there are also thousands of lesser known organic intellectuals who organize and lead movements for social change at the local level. So while organic intellectuals of the dominant classes work to support the existing hegemony, organic intellectuals of subordinate social groups act as change agents working against the hegemonic social order. Examples of organic intellectuals of subordinate groups are the leaders, advisors, organizers, and writers who serve feminist, civil rights, environmental, and other social activist groups.

In addition to their organizational and leadership roles, another important function of progressive organic intellectuals is to assimilate traditional intellectuals and enlist them in social change projects.[39] Traditional intellectuals have important skills, resources, and institutional locations that give them, potentially, significant cultural, ideological, and organizational power. If they are not enlisted in

---

38. Gramsci, 5.
39. Ibid., 10.

progressive causes, they may become the kind of "accommodating intellectuals" who, despite their attempts to remain objective and "professional," serve the status quo by default. Or they might become fully incorporated into the existing hegemonic order as active agents in its maintenance and reproduction.[40]

Intellectuals, Ideology, and Social Change

As progressive social groups develop organic intellectuals, these intellectuals provide the focus and direction necessary for their groups to organize as movements. They do this, in part, through their articulation of alternative ideologies. Alternative ideologies create new understandings of the social world, and new visions that help mobilize people to struggle for social change.

Gramsci makes the point that *all* members of society have certain intellectual capacities, which they utilize in varying degrees in their work and in other spheres of their daily lives. Individuals use their intellectual abilities to understand and evaluate common conceptions of the social world and govern their participation in social life. They can either go along with dominant social conceptions and practices, or challenge them and seek to change them. The task for progressive social groups then, is to develop the critical intellectual capacities of every one of their group members, to develop each member as a potential leader—an organic intellectual—who will create new, liberating conceptions of the world and work with others to bring them into existence.[41]

The idea of "organic" intellectuals "refers both to the relation of intellectuals [as leaders and organizers] to the classes in whose behalf they speak, and to the breakdown of the distinction between leaders and the led."[42] Since any member of a social group has the intellectual capability to play a social and political leadership role, anyone can potentially become an organic intellectual, working to expand American democracy. This is an egalitarian conception of

---

40. Stanley Aronowitz and Henry Giroux, *Education under Siege* (London: Routledge and Kegan Paul, 1987), 39.

41. Gramsci, 9.

42. Stanley Aronowitz, "The Future of Socialism?" in *Social Text* 24 (1990): 106.

intellectuals and of political leadership. It contrasts sharply with other views, whether conservative, liberal or left, which see intellectuals as a natural elite, separate from, and above common people.

Gramsci's concept of organic intellectuals is central to a theory of the process of radical democratic social change. Organic intellectuals of subordinate groups can organize cultural and political struggle for a new hegemonic order based on principles of justice, freedom for the self-development of all, and a radical, public democracy in which "every citizen can govern."[43]

The Importance of Education

In order to serve the needs of advanced capitalism, American society has had to create at least a minimally educated and trained general workforce, as well as large numbers of technically specialized intellectuals, and intellectuals of the managerial and directive type. It has also been necessary to socialize these workers and intellectuals to accept an ideology of privatized democracy that justifies or makes allowances for the relations of domination, inequality, and injustice inherent in American capitalist society.

The primary institution for training and socializing workers and intellectuals is the education system.[44] The extensive U.S. system of public and private schools, from elementary through university level, serves the educational and ideological purposes of the American social status quo. However, it also offers possibilities for initiating ideological and social change.

One possible source of social change lies in the fact that, as Althusser states, schools are contested ideological terrain. This means that efforts by the dominant social groups to educate and socialize a compliant workforce are likely to meet resistance. Students may reject the best-laid plans and programs offered by a school. Of course, as Paul Willis demonstrates in *Learning to Labor*, students' resistance to official school culture and expectations can itself be incorporated into the dynamic process of young people's socialization to working-class jobs and working-class lives.[45] So student

---

43. Gramsci, 40.
44. Gramsci, 10.
45. Paul Willis, *Learning to Labor* (New York: Columbia University Press, 1981).

resistance to school culture does not alone guarantee the formation of a counterhegemonic social movement. Still, the fact that young people can and do draw on their own cultures and knowledge to resist socialization to the dominant order, raises the possibility that their resistance could be organized to support public democratic ideals. This could happen if some young people among them received the support and guidance, either inside the school or outside, to nurture their intellectual development along critical, activist lines. These young people could become progressive organic intellectuals and take on leadership roles among progressive social groups.

Another pool of potential social change agents is created as a byproduct of one of the most basic functions of the American educational system—educating the managers and technicians who will run American business and government. In order to generate a cohort of highly qualified intellectuals to manage the machinery of the social order, it is necessary to create a relatively large pool of highly educated and trained people from which the system-serving intellectuals can be drawn. The selectiveness of the process means that many who receive a fairly high level of intellectual training will not—or at least will not at all times—be incorporated into the types of positions for which they have been trained.

Such a selection process "creates the possibility of vast crises of unemployment [and underemployment] for the middle intellectual strata, and in all modern societies this actually takes place."[46] The underutilization of a large cohort of intellectuals is potentially very dangerous for the existing social order. These intellectuals could become a source of leadership for movements of resistance and struggle for social change.[47] What prevents this from happening in many cases is the demobilizing power of American hegemonic ideologies of democracy, which encourage individualistic, privately oriented activities at the expense of public democratic action.

The question that arises is, who can provide the support and guidance to help develop a counterhegemonic consciousness and public activist stance among students and alienated adults?

---

46. Ibid., 11.

47. Ibid., 11. It is interesting that conservative economist Joseph Schumpeter elaborates on precisely the same problem in his classic book on capitalist political economy. See Joseph Schumpeter, *Capitalism, Socialism and Democracy* (New York: Harper Torchbooks, 1950, orig. 1942), 152–55.

One source of counterhegemonic leadership in society can be found outside the schools, among the numerous social activist movements and groups, some of which are working consciously to expand American democracy. These include such groups as feminists; civil rights organizations; community-based organizations; groups organized around the social, cultural, and political concerns of people of color; and environmentalists. As will be discussed later, such groups can provide spaces in which young people and others can learn to understand critically the ideologies and the concrete injustices of the hegemonic social and political order, and organize to challenge it.

The current battle for a counterhegemonic vision and practice of public democracy has been joined on many cultural and ideological fronts. Some of the groups in this struggle have understood that it is not enough to fight strictly for greater political power. They have come to realize, following Gramsci, that the only way to create an expanded public democracy in which they can hold greater political power is by working to change American culture.

In addition to social activist organizations of feminists, people of color, environmentalists, and others outside of education, the other key site for the struggle for a new hegemony of public democracy is *inside* the public education system. Within the contested ideological terrain of schools, committed progressive teachers can take on roles as organic intellectuals—as public, transformative intellectuals "who combine . . . thinking and practice with a political project grounded in the struggle for a culture of liberation and justice."[48] They can fight for control of their own workplaces, the schools, in order to transform them from institutions of ideological and social reproduction into places where teachers and students examine dominant ideologies and existing social relations from critical, ethical perspectives.[49] Such work helps develop young people's capacities for critical thinking. It can also lead students to formulate alternative visions of society, and begin to take action to realize those visions. An educational process such as this would be a powerful preparation

---

48. Stanley Aronowitz and Henry Giroux, *Postmodern Education* (Minneapolis: University of Minnesota Press, 1991), 109; see also Aronowitz and Giroux, *Education under Siege* (London: Routledge and Kegan Paul, 1986), 36–37.

49. Aronowitz and Giroux, *Postmodern Education*, 108–10.

for students, as young, organic intellectuals who could themselves join the struggle for a new public democracy.

The image of the United States as a world model—a beacon of democracy—is at the center of an ideology that partially masks the systemic relations of domination and subordination, the inequalities and injustices of American society. The dominant American ideology of liberal, republican democracy, together with its associated, sharply limited practices of democracy, encourages people to accept as natural, commonsense realities the continued existence and recent exacerbation of vast inequalities in every area of social life. The project of articulating a radical, participatory, and public vision of democracy and struggling to bring it about is the most important counterhegemonic project that can be undertaken in the United States today.

As Althusser and Gramsci argue, the conflict between established ideological conceptions and practices and alternative ones, takes place in the political, legal, and especially the cultural arenas of society. Much of the struggle to establish a new hegemonic order, under new ideological conceptions and practices of democracy, goes on through the work of feminist, environmental, African-American, Latino, Asian-American, and other organized subordinate social groups. Organic intellectuals play an important role here, organizing people to support these counterhegemonic democratic projects.

Meanwhile, the educational system, as a key apparatus for ideological production and for training intellectuals, is one of the most important sites for the struggle over ideas and practices of democracy. Public education, the one public institution specifically charged with preparing young people to become full members of society, can play a central role in the formation of young people's understandings of democracy, and of themselves as citizens in a democracy. In their function of helping students develop their intellectual abilities, schools also strongly influence the ability of young people to participate intelligently and effectively in a democracy.

Public schools are, literally, instruments of the state. Since the state, and its schools, are instruments of the established social order, it might seem futile to look to schools as possible instruments for challenging dominant understandings and practices of democracy. But if hegemony is understood as a dynamic process, and if schools are seen as sites of ideological contestation, then it is possible that there is a "transformative role that schools can play in advancing the democratic possibilities inherent in the existing society."[50] Educators who seek to play such a role must engage young people in projects of study, dialogue, and action that will enable them to begin to reconstruct the current hegemonic ideology of democracy along more participatory, public, egalitarian, and just lines.

Before beginning a discussion of how educators might engage students in public democratic study and action, it is necessary first to explore the raw material of such a project. It is important to examine closely two major strains of American democratic ideology and practice.

The first tradition sees democracy as a privately oriented, individualistic system with little room for most people to participate in self-rule. This tradition of *Federalist democracy* or *privatized democracy* is rooted in the political thought of Hobbes and Locke, the authors of the *Federalist Papers*, Adam Smith and the utilitarian liberals, and twentieth-century American pluralist theorists and free market economists.

The second tradition proposes an alternative vision and practice of democracy, grounded in the work of Rousseau, Jefferson, Dewey, Mills, and several important feminist theorists such as Carol Gould, Nancy Fraser, Carole Pateman, and Carol Gilligan. This tradition of *public democracy* sees people's participation in public life as the essential ingredient in democratic government.

It will be the task of the next three chapters to examine the main features of these two democratic traditions.

---

50. Henry Giroux, *Schooling and the Struggle for Public Life* (Minneapolis: University of Minnesota Press, 1988), 185.

CHAPTER 2

Ideological Roots of Privatized and Public Democracy

Contrasting Locke and the Federalists with Rousseau and Jefferson

Two major conceptions of American democracy have been at odds since the birth of the nation. The first, *privatized democracy*, has dominated American democratic thought and practice. The second tradition, *public democracy*, has nevertheless posed a constant challenge to privatized democratic thought. For educators who wish to join the struggle for a more participatory, more just democracy, it is necessary to understand the conflicting ideas that support these competing conceptions of American democracy.

The origin of both privatized and public conceptions of American democracy is the tradition of political philosophy known as liberalism. Liberalism has contributed much to the theory and practice of American democracy, from its initial assumptions about inalienable individual rights to the very structure and processes of the government that is intended to protect those rights. However, the dominance of the privatized strain of American political ideas and practice has come to inhibit our ability to understand society's problems, envision solutions, and take public action to solve them.

Locke and the Federalists

The men who formulated and worked to ratify the United States Constitution were ideological disciples of John Locke. They believed that people come together in political society for protection against constant exposure "to the invasions of others."[1] In this way, people effect the "mutual preservation of their lives, liberties, and estates," all of which Locke referred to by the general name, "property."[2] Since property was seen as the best buffer against life's insecurities, the acquisition of property was the fundamental human right, underlying the other rights of life and liberty. According to C. B. MacPherson, Locke's theory of labor, value, and property so elevates the importance of property rights that "the individual right of appropriation overrides any moral claims of the society."[3] For MacPherson, this idea is one of the central tenets of the ideology of "possessive individualism" that lies at the heart of Lockean liberalism.

Following Locke's reasoning, the American founders designed a constitutional government and later a Bill of Rights around the need to protect two guiding principles: the individual right of appropriation (i.e., the pursuit of property) and individual liberty.

The founders thought they could best protect these liberties through a federalist, republican government. It is to the founders' great credit that the government they created provided for formal protections of many fundamental individual liberties, such as freedom of religion, freedom of speech, expression, and the press, and freedom from various kinds of incursions by the state into people's private lives.[4]

However, they were quite clear about their antipathy toward direct democracy, for two reasons. First, they believed it could not be practiced on the scale of a large nation-state. Second, they harbored fears about the people's ability to govern itself, without threatening

---

1. John Locke, *Second Treatise on Government: An Essay Concerning the True Original Extent and End of Civil Government*, ch. 9, pt. 123, in *Social and Political Philosophy*, ed. John Somerville and Ronald E. Santoni (Garden City, NY: Anchor Books, Doubleday and Co., 1963), 184.

2. Locke, ch. 9, pt. 123, 184.

3. C. B. MacPherson, *The Political Theory of Possessive Individualism* (London: Oxford University Press, 1962), 220–21.

4. Tragically, these protections of individual liberties were not extended to all who lived in the United States. Generations of black slaves, women, and Native Americans were specifically excluded from these protections.

established property relations, which they believed arose from natural differences in people's abilities to acquire property.

In *The Federalist Papers*, Alexander Hamilton, James Madison, and John Jay expounded their views on the virtues of the U.S. Constitution. James Madison in particular laid out some of the chief threats posed by popular government to property and liberty, and the remedies that he believed the Constitution provided against those threats.[5] He carefully contrasted the problems caused by direct democracy with the solutions available in the indirect democracy of federalist, republican (representative) government.

Among other things, Madison argued that the institutions and practices of a representative, federalist republic would protect against "a rage for paper money, for an abolition of debts, for an equal division of property, or for any other improper or wicked project."[6] It is worth noting that his examples of improper, wicked projects were all projects that would threaten established monied or propertied interests.

The Federalist Papers demonstrate that one of Madison's primary concerns was to protect individual property and liberty from violation either by the government, or by a faction of citizens who might use the government to trample the rights of others. Since direct popular participation in government was seen as a potential threat to individual property and liberty, it had to be limited and controlled. This was to be accomplished through the governmental institutions and political processes of U.S. federalism, which channeled popular participation, and constitutionally divided and diffused political power. Under this system, the role of citizens in their government would be limited chiefly to their right to vote for representatives who—it was hoped—would honestly and effectively carry out the actual business of government. The rest of the time, people would be left to their private, individualistic pursuit of property.

Contrasting Madison, Jefferson and Rousseau

Thomas Jefferson shared Madison's concern for protecting individual rights to property and liberty. He also recognized the threat

---

5. Alexander Hamilton, John Jay, and James Madison, *The Federalist Papers*, ed. Clinton Rossiter (New York: New American Library, 1961), especially no. 10 and nos. 47–51.
6. Ibid., 84.

to these rights that could arise through the abuse of power in government. He believed that government should leave people, as much as possible, "free to regulate their own pursuits of industry and improvement."[7] For this reason, he agreed with Madison on the necessity of constitutional controls, including separation of powers, to prevent the concentration of power in any one branch of government.[8] However, an important difference in their thinking arose around this point—the need to protect against abuse of power in government.

Madison seemed content to rely on the mechanisms of constitutional government to protect against the corruption of power. In his view, the government, with its separation of powers, would keep itself in check and avoid the illegitimate amassing of power. Madison's major concern was in keeping the direct influence of the people out of government, for he saw their extensive participation as a chief source of government corruption. In short, Madison exhibited a profound mistrust of the people.

Jefferson had a very different view. His main fear was of leaving the government to look after itself, even if there were constitutional checks in place. Jefferson believed that

> every government degenerates when trusted to the rulers of the people alone. The people themselves are its only safe depositories. And to render even them safe their minds must be improved to a certain degree.[9]

So while Madison sought to protect the government from the people, Jefferson believed that the people were the only ones who could guarantee that the government would not become corrupted. Madison assumed that involving the people too much in the political process would automatically awaken dangerous "public passions."[10] But Jefferson envisioned a highly interactive relationship between government and citizens. The government should work

---

7. Thomas Jefferson, *Crusade Against Ignorance: Thomas Jefferson on Education*, ed. Gordon C. Lee (New York: Teachers College Press, 1966), 53.

8. Thomas Jefferson, *Notes on the State of Virginia*, ed. William Peden, (W. W. Norton and Co., 1982, orig. 1787), 120.

9. Jefferson, *Notes on Virginia*, 148.

10. *The Federalist Papers*, no. 49, 313–15.

purposefully to educate the public's ability to reason; and the citizens, in turn, would apply reason in the numerous aspects of their participation in government. Jefferson explained that this relationship between government and citizens would take the form of a complex social process, which would guard against corruption and abuse of power. He understood this process as follows.

Jefferson believed that people possessed different kinds and degrees of talent. Those who rose to the top of society due to their virtuous efforts and natural talents formed a "natural aristocracy."[11] The natural aristocracy benefitted society through its overall leadership and its service in government. Jefferson believed that there was also an artificial aristocracy, based on wealth and the social position into which people were born. He saw this artificial aristocracy as a corrupting influence in society, and especially in government. Jefferson believed this artificial aristocracy would try to use its wealth and social connections to get into positions of political power, where it would presumably do political "mischief," abusing its power and threatening the public's liberty and property.

Jefferson proposed to limit the artificial aristocracy's ability to acquire political power in three ways. First, he intended that the electoral process itself would give voters the opportunity to judge the worthiness of candidates for government office. Voters would then choose members of the natural aristocracy of the talented and virtuous for government office, over the artificial aristocracy of the wealthy.[12] This was comparable to Madison's reliance on citizens to vote into government people of wisdom and public virtue.[13] But Jefferson didn't wish simply to rely on the mechanism of an electoral filter against interested majority passions. He intended, instead, to educate citizens so that they might better recognize the public interest and protect their rights.

Thus Jefferson's second approach to the problem was a proposed law to establish a system of mass public education in his home state of Virginia. This proposed system called for free elementary education

---

11. Jefferson, *Crusade against Ignorance*, 162.
12. Ibid., 163.
13. *The Federalist Papers*, no. 10, 82–84.

for all white male children.[14] The purpose of this level of education was explicitly to prepare citizens to participate intelligently in representative government. They would study, especially, history, to

> avail them of the experience of other times and other nations; . . . qualify them as judges of the designs of men; . . . enable them to know ambition under every disguise it may assume; and knowing it, to defeat its views.

Education would thereby render "the people the safe, as they are the ultimate, guardians of their own liberty."[15] According to Jefferson, this level of education was intended, ultimately, "to instruct the mass of our citizens in these, their rights, interests and duties, as men and citizens."[16]

Elementary education would be followed by continued free education through the university level for those boys from poor families who demonstrated great talent and hard work at their studies. Wealthier families could also put their boys through this educational system, as long as they were willing to pay the tuition.[17] Through this proposed system of public education, Jefferson hoped to prepare the "aristocracy" of ability to compete successfully with the aristocracy of wealth for positions of leadership in government and civil society.

Jefferson's third approach to the problem of the disproportionate access of the wealthy to political power was a legislative effort at direct, though limited, economic redistribution. Jefferson wrote and gained passage of two laws in Virginia which worked to disperse

---

14. Like the other American founders, Jefferson did not intend women, Native Americans, or blacks to exercise the rights of citizens. For this reason, he did not envision their participation in public education. Although Jefferson himself was a slave owner, he proposed legislation several times that would have abolished slavery in the state of Virginia. See Jefferson, *Notes on Virginia*, 137, 6n. These proposals, like his proposal for public education, were never passed.

Clearly there were deep contradictions between Jefferson's ideas on wide participation in democracy, and his failure to promote citizenship or education for women, blacks, or Native Americans. Nevertheless, despite its reprehensible omissions, Jefferson's proposal for public education was significant, as one of the country's first calls for widespread education for democratic citizenship. It established a principle which could be extended by later, more inclusive public democratic theorists.

15. Ibid., 148.

16. Jefferson, *Crusade*, 117.

17. Jefferson, *Notes*, 147.

hereditary fortunes over a period of generations. He felt that these laws "laid the ax to the foot of the pseudo-aristocracy."[18]

Besides these ideas for undercutting the influence of the wealthy in government, Jefferson proposed several other measures to enhance popular participation in government. First, he proposed legislation to divide up the state of Virginia into a system of small wards. These wards were to be "little republics," self-governing over many local matters such as roads, law enforcement, care of the poor, and so forth. Most significantly, the ward system would provide a mechanism for direct popular participation in the governing of the state. As Jefferson envisioned it, "a general call of ward meetings by their wardens on the same day through the State, would at any time produce the genuine sense of the people on any required point, and would enable the State to act in mass, as [the people of Massachusetts] have so often done . . . by their town meetings."[19]

In addition, Jefferson believed that when there was a publicly felt need to change a government's constitution, or to correct abuses of it, the people could be called upon to elect delegates to resolve the problem through a constitutional convention. A convention would be called whenever two of the three branches of government voted with two–thirds of their members to do so.[20] Madison explicitly rejected this idea, for fear that dangerous public passions would be aroused.[21]

Jefferson also favored universal (white) male suffrage, as a means of minimizing the potential for elections, and government, to be corrupted. He therefore wrote universal free manhood suffrage into his proposed draft of a new constitution for Virginia.[22] He explained his reasoning on this question as follows.

> The influence over government must be shared among all the people. If every individual which composes their mass participates of the ultimate authority, the government will be safe; because the corrupting of the whole mass will exceed any private resources of wealth. . . . It has been thought that corruption

18. Jefferson, *Crusade*, 164.
19. Ibid., 164–65.
20. Jefferson, *Notes*, 221.
21. *The Federalist Papers*, no. 49.
22. Jefferson, *Notes*, 211.

is restrained by confining the right of suffrage to a few of the wealthier of the people: but it would be more effectually restrained by an extension of that right to such numbers as would bid defiance to the means of corruption."[23]

Jefferson had a fairly simplistic understanding of the potential for corrupting or manipulating the electoral process. He was perhaps unable to imagine the enormous amassing of corporate and individual wealth in the twentieth century, which, in combination with the rise of the centrality of mass media in elections, has created a large market for the purchase of influence in government. Nevertheless, his proposed remedies for the tendencies toward corruption in government suggest an important constant in his thinking on democracy: Jefferson believed in the need to involve the people actively in the day-to-day business of their government and public life.

Again, this was in stark contrast to the spirit of Madison's thought on popular participation. It also ran counter to the practice in most states at the time, in which there were substantial property requirements attached to voter eligibility.[24]

Based on this review of Jefferson's ideas on the relationship between citizens and government, it is clear that he accepted and championed the basic liberal principles of protection of property and liberty through representative republican government. However, he envisioned a far more extensive role of the people in such a government, including a significant degree of direct popular participation, than did James Madison or other key liberals of his time. Jefferson, in contrast to Madison, had a deep faith in the potential, indeed the necessity, for common people to participate actively in their government and ensure that it served the public interest.

In this regard, Jefferson echoed some of the themes that Jean-Jacques Rousseau articulated in *The Social Contract*. For example, Rousseau stressed the importance of reason, and especially the development of public reason, to enable a society to create a public

---

23. Ibid., 149.
24. In *Notes on Virginia* for example, Jefferson listed that state's property requirements for eligibility: ownership of 100 uninhabited acres, or 25 acres with a house, or a house or lot in a town. Ibid., 118.

good.[25] Jefferson recognized the importance of this idea, and attempted to implement it by proposing a system of public schooling for the state of Virginia that would educate the people and train their ability to reason, not only to protect their individual rights and interests, but also to inform their public duties as citizens. This system of education would help develop citizens' watchfulness over government, to protect against deception, corruption, and potential infringements on liberty. But it would also inform and train people to contemplate public issues and public actions; it would sharpen people's ability to choose good leaders; and it would serve to develop good leaders from among the people at large.

Jefferson, like Madison, was not an advocate of direct democracy, either as practiced by the ancient Greeks or as championed by Rousseau. Jefferson, with Madison, simply didn't believe it could be practiced on a scale beyond that of a town.[26] They both favored representative democracy as a means of extending the principal of popular rule over a large nation. This puts both at odds with Rousseau, who believed that representative government was entirely incompatible with democracy, because for him, the people's "sovereignty cannot be represented."[27]

Nevertheless, Jefferson, with his faith in the participation of the people, was a good deal closer to the spirit of Rousseau's thought than was Madison, who feared their participation. Jefferson's reliance on the people to resolve constitutional problems and abuses—albeit indirectly, through representative constitutional conventions—was very much in line with Rousseau's faith in assemblies of the people as "the shield of the body politic and the brake on the government."[28] Jefferson's desire for universal white manhood suffrage was also, within the representative form of government, akin to Rousseau's belief in the critical importance of the participation of all citizens in the business of the state.[29]

---

25. Jean-Jacques Rousseau, *The Social Contract* (New York: Penguin Books, 1985, orig. published 1762), 83.

26. Jefferson, "Letter to Isaac A. Tiffany," in *Social and Political Philosophy*, ed. John Somerville and Ronald Santoni (Garden City, NY: Anchor Books, 1963), 280.

27. Rousseau, 141.

28. Ibid., 139.

29. Ibid., 140.

Jefferson and Rousseau were also of a similar mind in their fear of people's tendency to pursue private interests at the expense of their participation in public affairs. For both of them, this posed a serious threat to the well-being of democratic government. Thus Jefferson warned:

> [People] will forget themselves, but in the sole faculty of making money, and will never think of uniting to effect a due respect for their rights.[30]

Rousseau likewise stated:

> It is the bustle of commerce and the crafts, it is the avid thirst for profits . . . that commute personal service [in public affairs] for money.[31]

Rousseau felt that if citizens became so involved in the pursuit of private gain that they could not participate in their government and public affairs, this would mark the downfall of democratic government and the beginning of tyranny.

> As soon as someone says of the business of the state—"What does it matter to me?"—then the state must be reckoned lost.[32]

For Rousseau, the problem came down to the exercise of sovereignty. If citizens did not take an active role in expressing their will on public affairs and participating in government, then "the silence of the people permits the assumption that the people consent."[33] Whatever government leaders chose to do would be seen as a legitimate representation of the general will.

Jefferson was also aware of another problem that greatly concerned Rousseau—the corrosive effect of economic inequality on political equality, and on the possibilities, therefore, for freedom and self-government.[34] Jefferson's proposal for a system of public education, along with his inheritance legislation, reflected practical attempts to mitigate the effects of economic inequality. His proposed education

---

30. Jefferson, *Notes*, 161.
31. Rousseau, 140.
32. Rousseau, 141.
33. Rousseau, 70.
34. Rousseau, 96–97.

system's main purpose was to thwart the ability of the artificial aristocracy of the wealthy to corrupt the government. His inheritance laws seemed to follow directly from Rousseau's prescription for limiting the extremes of inequality through legislation.

So even though Jefferson was a devoted disciple of liberal, representative democracy, he had an inkling of its internal contradictions. He recognized that the democratic ideals of political equality and public participation could come into conflict with the tendencies in liberalism toward economic inequality, and toward the abandonment of public life.

These contradictions have affected the conduct of political life in the United States in several ways. First, liberal thought, and the material reality of life in liberal society, tell people that they must seek the fulfillment of their most basic needs in the private sphere. Indeed, the very ideas of liberty and individual rights, as has been shown, are intimately linked to the pursuit of private property. Thus, as Jefferson understood, there are strong incentives for people to abandon the public sphere in pursuit of private gain. Second, the pursuit of private gain leads inevitably to economic inequality. As Jefferson well knew, economic inequality leads to political inequality, as the wealthy exercise inordinate political influence. Third, economic inequality creates obstacles to the participation of middle- and low-income citizens in the public sphere. For as struggling middle- and low-income people must toil ever harder in the private sphere in pursuit of their material survival and security, they have less time and energy to devote to public life.

Because Jefferson had a sense of these contradictions, if not a fully elaborated understanding of them, he was concerned about the wealthy pseudo-aristocracy and its corrupting influence on government. That is why he proposed so many measures to counter their power and minimize their influence; and why he argued repeatedly the need to maximize popular participation in government and public life.[35] That is also why he insisted on the need to educate people to be citizens and future government leaders: to keep the public

---

35. Jefferson, "Letter to John Taylor," in *Social and Political Philosophy*, ed. Somerville and Santoni, 252–54. Also, Jefferson, *Writings*, 1380, cited in Francis Moore Lappe, *Rediscovering America's Values* (New York: Ballantine Books, 1989), 198.

sphere alive, honest, and effective in the face of forces that would impede it.

Madison and the other writers of the *Federalist Papers*, for their part, also understood that economic liberalism led to economic inequality. But they viewed such inequality as inevitable, arising from the exercise of individual liberty. By implication, they were willing to accept a significant degree of political inequality (arising from economic inequality) to protect the right to unequal acquisition of property. That is why Madison was so concerned about minimizing popular participation in government, to prevent the propertyless masses from instituting "wicked projects" of egalitarian politics. He offered an institutional view of the proper functioning of government, in which constitutional structures and mechanisms would protect against the excesses of popular demands as well as against the abuse of power in government. Although these institutional mechanisms have historically acted as checks and balances to rein in some serious abuses of government power, the limitations they have placed on popular participation have also systematically discouraged individuals from taking an active role in their government and public life.

Despite their shared foundations in liberal thought, Federalist and Jeffersonian democratic ideas represent sharply divergent trends in American political thought—trends that have been at odds since the founding of the U.S. republic. Federalist ideas have formed the foundation for current conceptions of privatized democracy. Jeffersonian ideas have been the precursors of public democratic ideas. In the nineteenth and twentieth centuries, the thinking and practice implied in each of these competing visions of democracy have taken on newer and more complex forms.

The following chapter will examine two of the later developments of liberal political theory—utilitarianism and pluralism. These political ideologies have reinforced the basic tendencies of privatized democracy, and deepened their imprint on American political institutions and practices. The chapter will conclude with a discussion of how consumer culture, traditional democratic participation patterns (especially voting), and the capitalist economic context of American society, have all supported the continuing hegemony of privatized democracy.

CHAPTER 3

Privatized Democracy

Nineteenth- and Twentieth-Century Ideology and Practice

Today most Americans experience democracy as the freedom to earn money and buy things. Democracy has come to mean simply our ability to compete freely for a job, and then use our income to secure life's necessities, along with whatever luxuries we can afford.

This economic understanding of democracy—nearly devoid of public, political content—has been shaped by a number of ideological and practical influences. Political theories of nineteenth- and twentieth-century utilitarianism and pluralism, building on earlier Federalist ideas, have combined with an ideology of mass consumerism to influence today's dominant conceptions of American democracy. In addition, historical patterns of limited voting eligibility, along with other constraints on democratic participation imposed by the workings of American capitalism, have also helped shape people's understandings and practices of democracy. This chapter examines in some detail these influences on American democracy.

Utilitarianism

Utilitarianism is a social and political philosophy that gained prominence during the nineteenth century with the writings of Jeremy

Bentham, James Mill, and John Stuart Mill. Utilitarian theory is founded on several of the basic assumptions of federalist democratic ideology, including the following:

1. Individuals are essentially equal in their liberties and rights.
2. Individuals are motivated by self-interest and they pursue their self-interest rationally. (As noted earlier, this self-interest generally takes the form of material or property interests.)
3. Individuals desire freedom, defined as an absence of external constraints on their pursuit of self-interest.[1]

Utilitarianism starts with these assumptions, but goes further, to formulate explicitly some ideas that are only implicit in federalist ideology. Utilitarians define individual self-interest as pleasure or happiness. The community or society is considered an artificial aggregate of individuals, formed to facilitate its members' free pursuit of their self-interest. The general interest of the community is understood as simply the sum of the interests of the individual members who make up the society.[2] Therefore the best society is defined as the one that provides the greatest balance of pleasure over pain for the greatest number of individuals.[3]

---

1. Carol Gould, *Rethinking Democracy* (New York: Cambridge University Press, 1988), 92–93. Gould calls the theory that is based on these assumptions liberal individualism. She considers Locke, Jefferson, Bentham, and James and John Stuart Mill as an undifferentiated group of liberal individualist thinkers. She opposes this group to pluralist thinkers, examples of whom she identifies as Madison, Dewey, Schumpeter, Dahl, and Berelson. Presumably, the key point of differentiation between these two groups is whether they conceive of political actors as individuals or as groups.

I have a different scheme for differentiating these theorists. I believe that all those whom she mentions trace their roots back to the liberal individualist tradition of Locke. However, I find the crucial defining characteristic to be not whether they understand political participation as an individualistic or a group phenomenon; but rather how they understand the public sphere, and the proper nature and extent of popular participation in it. It is based on this distinction that I group Madison and the utilitarians Bentham, James Mill, and John Stuart Mill with the pluralists Schumpeter, Berelson, and Schattschneider; and I group Jefferson with Dewey, C. Wright Mills, Robert Dahl (especially in his later work), and recent participatory democratic theorists such as Carole Pateman, Benjamin Barber, and Carol Gould herself. I discuss several of these theorists in Chapter 4.

2. Frances Moore Lappe, *Rediscovering America's Values* (New York: Ballantine Books, 1989), 8.

3. Bertrand Russell, *A History of Western Philosophy*, (New York: Touchstone Books, 1972), 775. See also John Plamenatz, *The English Utilitarians* (Oxford: Basil Blackwell and

Bentham, James Mill, and John Stuart Mill were all strong proponents of democracy in their era. Indeed, in his later writings Bentham called for radical democratic reform of British government. All three men favored universal suffrage within a framework of representative government. At first glance, then, it would seem that these utilitarians were champions of the public life of participation in democratic government. However, John Stuart Mill's work, especially *Representative Government* and *On Liberty*, can be read as highly mistrustful of placing government in the hands of a participating public.

In *Representative Government*, Mill, to an even greater degree than the American Federalists, constructed a scheme of government around institutions and political practices intended to buffer government from the possible democratic excesses of the unenlightened masses. These mechanisms included the establishment of a professional, expert administrative service and an expert Legislative Commission; a system of proportional representation to guarantee representation of political minorities; bicameral legislatures; and plural voting based on intellectual ability.[4] In *On Liberty*, Mill made a powerful argument for the primacy of individualism and the personal freedoms of private life over the rights of government or society to interfere or impose its will.

The point here is not that Mill's principles on limiting the excesses of popular opinion or the reach of government into private life are misguided. Indeed, certain of Mill's well-argued principles supporting minority rights and non-interference in private life are welcome resources for progressives in today's political climate. These principles can be used in political struggles for protection of the rights of gays and lesbians, women's right to safe and legal abortion, and the rights of immigrants and people of color to equal opportunities in education, employment, and housing.

Mott, Ltd., 1966). For relevant readings of the primary texts, see Jeremy Bentham, *A Bentham Reader*, ed. Mary Peter Mack (New York: Pegasus, 1969); John Stuart Mill, *Utilitarianism, with Critical Essays*, ed. Samuel Gorovitz (New York: Bobbs-Merrill, 1971); John Stuart Mill, *Representative Government*, ed. Currin V. Shields, (New York: Bobbs-Merrill, 1958).

4. J. H. Burns, "Utilitarianism and Democracy," in J. S. Mill, *Utilitarianism with Critical Essays*, ed. Samuel Gorovitz (New York: Bobbs-Merrill, 1971), 270.

The problem, however, is that the utilitarians' fear of democratic excesses can, and has been used to support an ideology which has devalued all of public life, and democratic participation itself. This tendency has been strengthened by the connection between political utilitarianism and the ideology of classical free market economics.

John Dewey has argued that utilitarian social thought is closely related to laissez-faire economic theory. This theory enshrines as "natural laws" several key propositions: that self-interest leads individuals to work and this produces wealth; that delaying gratification leads to creation of capital and production of greater wealth; that the market is regulated by an equilibrium rule of supply and demand. These "natural laws," coordinated by the invisible hand of Providence, ultimately work to the benefit of everyone, and thus of society. Since the social system is supposedly regulated by natural laws, politics and government are seen as unnatural, imperfect add-ons to society. Their role, therefore, should be strictly limited.[5]

Indeed, those who developed liberal and utilitarian economic and social theory were reacting in large part against established, oppressive government structures and practices. As Dewey said, "they were activated by a desire to reduce [government] to a minimum so as to limit the evil it could do."[6] The role of government for utilitarian free market economists, then, was simply to allow these natural laws to work, as well as to enforce contracts and protect property relations. Thus in this strain of utilitarian theory, the pursuit of pleasure or good was to take place almost entirely in the private, economic sphere. The representative mechanisms of the political system were assumed to be sufficient to adjudicate among clashing individual interests and to produce policies that would keep the economic system functioning properly. This, in turn, would produce the individual pleasures or goods that would add up to the society's total good. Widespread popular political activity, especially if it sought to challenge or in any way limit private pursuit of economic gain, was seen as an "unnatural" threat to the "natural" laws of liberal economics and utilitarian politics. It was to be avoided, or at

---

5. John Dewey, *The Public and Its Problems* (Chicago: Swallow Press, 1988, orig. 1927), 90–92.

6. Ibid., 86.

least controlled and limited as much as possible. In this view, the main goal of politics became system maintenance.[7]

Pluralism

Pluralism is a twentieth-century conceptualization which understands democratic politics as a process of competition among interest groups or parties. A few of the notable theorists of pluralism have been Joseph Schumpeter, David Truman, Robert Dahl (especially in his early writing), and E. E. Schattschneider. Pluralist explanations of American political practice have enjoyed wide acceptance among academics as well as in the broader social world.

Pluralism posits an essentially utilitarian model of social life, adding a few of its own key concepts. As in utilitarianism, individuals are seen as creatures whose most basic motivation is rationally to pursue their self-interest (pleasure or good) in the private sphere. However, individuals also belong to, or identify with groups, whose members share common material or ideological interests. These groups often become involved in public political activity based on their members' shared interests and views.

For pluralists, there are two main types of groups relevant to the political system: (1) interest groups; and (2) political parties. Interest groups seek to achieve their goals by influencing government officials, politicians, or public opinion. Political parties seek to achieve their ideological and material interests by sponsoring candidates for elections to public office; and by formulating policy positions and overall platforms upon which these candidates run, and if elected, attempt to govern.

Although some pluralist theorists imply that most, if not all citizens belong to groups that can at least potentially become active in exerting influence in the political process, others believe that most people rarely participate so directly.[8] E. E. Schattschneider in

---

7. Kalman Silvert, *The Reason for Democracy* (New York: Viking Press, 1976), 31–32.

8. David B. Truman takes the first position, that most citizens belong to interest groups. See Truman, *The Governmental Process: Political Interests and Public Opinion* (New York: Alfred A. Knopf, 1951), 34–37. The second position, that most people usually do not participate directly in interest group politics, is taken by E. E. Schattschneider, in *The Semi-Sovereign People* (Hinsdale, IL: Dryden Press, 1975, orig. 1960), and by Joseph Schumpeter, in *Capitalism, Socialism and Democracy* (New York: Harper & Row, third edition, 1962, orig. 1942).

particular offers evidence that strongly supports the claim that most people, and especially lower-income people, do not generally participate in interest-group politics.[9] Instead, these theorists believe that the most important aspect of the political process is the organization of political competition by political parties. Most people, if they are going to participate, enter the political process only to support specific candidates (and thus the policy platforms) that the parties offer. According to these theorists, *citizens in a modern democracy are not, and cannot be self-governing.* Citizens participate in the political conflict of elections by voting, and government and policy are byproducts of the competition.[10]

This view of citizen participation has become not only descriptive, but also prescriptive. It has come to define the ideal of the democratic process, and in so doing, has also defined the limits of democratic participation. The right to choose leaders from among those offered by the organized political parties, along with the existence of organized elite groups that pressure government to serve their interests, are now widely viewed as the defining characteristics of democracy. Although some theorists, such as Robert Dahl, are careful not to call such a system a democracy, in common parlance and understanding, the U.S. political system—a pluralist, low-participation republic—is a democracy.[11]

Through the theoretical reinforcement of utilitarianism and pluralism, American democracy has come to be conceived of largely in federalist democratic terms. Utilitarianism dissolves the concept of a public, societal good into a balance of pleasures and pains of all the individuals in society. But the pursuit of happiness or pleasure is to take place within the sphere of the "natural laws" of the economic world. As in the federalist view, then, any economic inequality that arises is viewed as natural, and is to be defended. The implication is that the political inequality which results from economic inequality is natural and acceptable.

---

9. E. E. Schattschneider, *The Semi-Sovereign People*, 32–35.

10. Schumpeter, 282; Schattschneider, 126, 133–34.

11. For Dahl, the U.S. political system, and many other modern representative systems, are "polyarchies." Dahl defines polyarchy as that collection of institutions which support the selection of leaders in representative "democracies." Robert Dahl, *Democracy and Its Critics* (New Haven: Yale University Press, 1989), 218–21.

In addition, politics, especially popular political activity, and even government itself, become suspect—seen as artificial social constructions outside of "natural" economic laws. This line of thinking reinforces the dual federalist fear of dangerous popular participation on the one hand, and the general mistrust of government on the other. The solution is also federalist: control and limit popular participation in politics, and rely as much as possible on the mechanisms of divided, representative government. Then keep tight constraints on most activities of government, in particular those that impinge in any way on the pursuit of property (profits) in the private sphere. Utilitarian thinking leads to the demise of the idea of the importance of popular political activity. Indeed, it pronounces a death sentence on the public sphere as a critical center of life in a democratic society.

Pluralism accepts utilitarianism's faith in the primacy of the economic realm in society, but also adapts the economic model to politics. It creates a model of political parties and interest groups competing in an open market for political power and influence in government. The propensity of economic inequality to lead to political inequality is not a major concern for pluralists, because politics is understood as essentially an elite activity. The people are demobilized politically, except for their voting activity, and the vote is thought of as a political resource shared equally by all. Pluralism does remove the concept of the public sphere from utilitarianism's death row, but only to remake it as spectacle, with most citizens as passive viewers.

Pluralist theory, building on utilitarian theory and based on federalist themes, acts as a powerful ideological constraint on people's conceptions of their role as participants in the public sphere. The public sphere becomes television—people are involved only in selecting the channel of a particular political candidate or party; after that they just watch. Pluralism offers a theory that explains and legitimizes the U.S. system of elite politics, ratified through the minimal popular participation of voting. It then pronounces this system the embodiment of democracy.

But the concept of "government of the people and by the people," has been emptied out of this idea of democracy. What we have instead is government of elites, by elites (through their interest groups and parties). The word democracy remains a patriotic slogan that

Americans revere as they revere the flag. But for most Americans the slogan has lost its Jeffersonian participatory and public meaning.

The passive, privately oriented vision of the role of citizens in U.S. democracy is further reinforced by several aspects of the interplay of consumer culture and U.S. political ideology and practice.

Consumer Culture and Ideology

Stuart Ewen has observed that the coming of a "culture of abundance" by the late nineteenth century allowed for "the flowering of a provocative, if somewhat passive, conception of democracy . . . *consumer democracy.*"[12] Mass production processes for the first time put colorful art images, stylish clothing, and other traditional symbols of privilege within the economic reach of the masses.[13] The result was the illusion of a growing egalitarianism in terms of people's material possessions. In fact, the system of industrial production that created the culture of abundance was predicated on the exploitation of workers and the maintenance of social inequality. Nevertheless, the symbolic egalitarianism created by the mass availability of consumer goods was seen as an important democratizing component in American society. Traditionally, those few people who enjoyed material privilege in any society were also the ones who monopolized political power. So when symbols of material egalitarianism became widespread in the United States, it was easy for people to associate those symbols with, and even substitute them for, the idea of the political egalitarianism of democracy.

This conceptualization of American democracy in consumer terms is perfectly synchronous with the ideas of federalist democracy. It offers a facsimile of material equality, thereby disguising economic inequality, and making it less likely to be held up as a cause of political inequality. It also encourages people to look to the economic sphere for substitute gratification of their desire for political equality. In this way it further devalues the idea of a vital public

---

12. Stuart Ewen, *All Consuming Images* (New York: Basic Books, 1988), 32.
13. Stuart Ewen and Elizabeth Ewen, "Images of Democracy," in *Channels of Desire: Mass Images and the Shaping of American Consciousness* (New York: McGraw-Hill, 1982), 169–82.

sphere where citizens might participate equally in the work of self-government.

This privatized, economic conception of democracy has continued to be an important mainstream ideological force in the United States. It was strongly reinforced by nearly fifty years of Cold War rhetoric. This rhetoric, emanating from political figures as well as from the advertising industry and the mass media more generally, constantly compared Soviet or Chinese Communism with American democracy. But such comparisons, couched in terms of Communism versus democracy, concealed more than they revealed. "Communism" is a term that was used to bring together both political and economic components of Soviet, East European and Chinese systems—they were one-party totalitarian political systems welded to state socialist economic systems. Similarly, the term "democracy" was used as a shorthand for the political and economic configuration of U.S. society—a system of two-party, representative government within a capitalist economic context.

The conflation of the economic and the political into the single terms, Communism and democracy, encouraged people to think of each term as representing a single, however muddled, idea. In the all-encompassing environment of Cold War propaganda, Communism became a code word for all that was evil and inferior; democracy for all that was good and superior. What was left was the vague sense that democracy had something to do with freedom, just as Communism had to do with unfreedom.

Given American society's enthrallment with consumerism, comparisons between Communism and democracy often ended up on economic grounds. Communism was always found wanting for its lack of freedom, but especially for its lack of consumer freedom due to its notoriously short supplies and limited varieties of quality consumer goods. Cold War ideology had set up the simplistic opposition between Communism and democracy. So by its logic democracy came to mean, for many people, simply freedom of choice in an abundant consumer's market.

Political Practice

This limited vision of democracy has been strengthened not only by the ideological trends I have been describing. It has also been reinforced by the fact that real opportunities to exercise democratic influence in U.S. politics have always been severely limited. For one thing, even the right to vote—supposedly the key to democracy, the one act of direct, regular public participation—has been seriously and systematically restricted throughout American history.[14] In addition, the capitalist context in which American politics operates creates few policy incentives that would encourage most middle- and low-income people to participate. It does create many material *dis*incentives to regular, active participation in public life. These pressures for nonparticipation are discussed in the remaining two sections of this chapter.

Voting Eligibility

At the time of the first U.S. presidential election in 1789, the right to vote was quite restricted in most states. Requirements that voters be property holders or taxpayers limited the electorate to some 50–75 percent of adult white males. Since adult white males were only about 20 percent of the total population, only about 10–15 percent of the population was eligible to vote that year.[15] Black men (both slaves and free men), Native American men, as well as all women, were categorically denied the right to vote.

White male and later black male suffrage were expanded dramatically during the nineteenth century, but as Piven and Cloward argue, votes were tightly controlled by political party organizations. Politics for most of this period remained focused on sectional, ethnic, and religious interests. This deflected mass political pressures from challenging elite interests.[16] Then in the late 1800s, elite interests did come under serious challenge from a mobilized and enfranchised radical populist movement. In 1896, business interests responded with massive financial and organizational support for Republican candidate William McKinley, enabling him to defeat

---

14. This has been true despite the gradual formal enfranchisement of adult citizens over time. See Piven and Cloward, *Why Americans Don't Vote* (New York: Pantheon, 1988).

15. Bruce Campbell, *The American Electorate* (New York: Holt, Rhinehart, Winston, 1979), 12–13.

16. Frances Fox Piven and Richard A. Cloward, *Why Americans Don't Vote* (New York: Pantheon Books, 1988), 27–41.

Democratic-Populist candidate William Jennings Bryan.[17] This victory for business interests was followed by a series of major electoral reforms, including new voter registration procedures. The effect of these reforms was to initiate a dramatic decline in electoral participation among low-income white voters.[18]

The demobilization of black voters took place through a separate process, but with an even more dramatic result. Black men had been guaranteed the right to vote with the Fifteenth Amendment to the Constitution in 1870. However, they were only able to exercise it relatively freely during the years of Reconstruction (and Union Army occupation) of the South. After that, their voting rights were nullified by a series of restrictions on voter eligibility, including poll taxes, property qualifications, literacy tests, and the system of the white primary, which excluded blacks from participation in Democratic primaries in Southern states. Since the South was effectively a one-party Democratic region for a hundred years after the Civil War, this last device virtually eliminated black influence in Southern electoral politics until the 1960s.[19]

Women received the right to vote in 1920. But they did so in the midst of the national trend toward demobilization of low-income voters. The result was that, for the most part, the only women who actually became voters were middle- and upper-class (white) women.

By the early twentieth century, according to Piven and Cloward, voter eligibility restrictions, "sharply reduced voting by the northern immigrant working class and virtually eliminated voting by southern blacks and poor whites."[20] Although the most blatant discriminatory eligibility requirements, such as the southern white primary, literacy tests and poll taxes were eliminated during the 1960s by the Voting Rights Act and the Twenty-fourth Amendment to the Constitution,[21] a complex system of obstacles to voter registration has remained largely in place in most states. This has had the effect of perpetuating a pattern of extremely low voter

17. Ibid., 46–51.
18. Ibid., 17–21, 53–56.
19. Edward S. Greenberg, *The American Political System: A Radical Approach*, third edition (Boston: Little, Brown and Co., 1983), 211–12.
20. Piven and Cloward, 6.
21. Bruce A. Campbell, *The American Electorate*, 31.

participation in the United States, a pattern which is especially prevalent among low-income and lesser-educated Americans.[22]

Piven and Cloward believe that the disenfranchisement of low-income and working-class voters has led the political parties to abandon both campaign rhetoric and policies that favor working-class interests. This, in turn, reinforces the alienation of low income people from politics. The political parties then defend the obstacles to voter registration to maintain the political status quo on which they have built their organizations.[23]

Thus the whole history of voter participation in the United States is one of seriously limited voting eligibility, through a variety of devices; and a resulting politics that has avoided challenges to elite interests. This is very much in keeping with the federalist reluctance to allow popular participation to threaten property or money interests. The result is that many people do not participate even in the basic political act of voting.[24]

Capitalist Political Economy and Non-participation

Other forces besides the politics of voting restrictions have contributed to the de-politicization of American citizenship. A key demobilizing force is the capitalist economic context that shapes American society and politics. In a capitalist democracy such as the United States, the society's well-being is entirely dependent on the well-being

---

22. Piven and Cloward, 17–18.

23. Ibid., 18–19.

24. Voter turnout for the 1988 presidential election was only about 50 percent of the U.S. voting-age population. This was the lowest turnout in a presidential election since 1924, and continued a steady decline which began in the 1964 election. See Richard Berke, "Experts Say Low 1988 Turnout May Be Repeated," *New York Times*, 13 November 1988. Even a significant increase in participation in the 1992 presidential election brought voter turnout to only 55% of the voting age population. See Robert Pear, "55% Voting Rate Reverses 30-Year Decline," *New York Times*, 5 November 1992. This of course means that even in an exceptionally high participation year, some 45% of the U.S. adult population did not vote in the presidential election.

In addition, in September 1990, Michael Oreskes reported on a study by the Times Mirror Center for the People and the Press that showed that political alienation is on the rise in the United States, and that this trend is especially strong among low- and middle-income people (defined as families earning less than $50,000 a year). Michael Oreskes, "Alienation from Government Grows, Poll Finds," *New York Times*, 19 September 1990.

of the capitalist economy. The maintenance of private profits is the condition for individual citizens' livelihoods (as workers), as well as for the material support of the very structure of government and whatever programs or services it would provide.[25] Therefore government officials are structurally bound to serve, or at least consider the needs of capital, as they formulate policies and programs. So proposed policies are always evaluated on the basis of their potential effects on corporate profits. This means that virtually any policy that proposes to provide a public good at the expense of corporate resources or freedoms, unless it offers clear benefits to corporate interests, faces an uphill battle for passage. In the United States, this produces a political landscape which is inherently sparse in its policy offerings for low-income and working people. Such a political landscape offers little to encourage the participation of these inactive citizens. The political alienation of these people is therefore further reinforced.

Moreover, since the economy's major investment decisions, upon which working people depend for their material security, are controlled by private capital, working people are always in a precarious economic condition. Because of this, they are forced to concern themselves primarily and continually with seeking material security in the private sphere, through higher wages, overtime work or second and third jobs.[26] With the decline in the power of organized labor, this is increasingly a private, individualistic struggle. Public sphere activity is always a lesser priority, unless there is a political issue that presents a tangible threat to the voters, such as the likelihood of higher taxes or the poisoning of the local environment.

In this way, capitalist democracy creates a needs structure geared toward the short-term pursuit of material needs.[27] Historically, American capitalist democracy has usually satisfied enough of the needs it has generated (while leaving enough insecurity) to discourage most people from abandoning the short term economic struggle for political struggle. As Joshua Cohen and Joel Rogers see it, "the structure of capitalist democracy thus effectively encourages the reduction of politics to striving over material gain."[28]

---

25. Joshua Cohen and Joel Rogers, *On Democracy: Toward a Transformation of American Society* (New York: Penguin Books, 1984), 53.
26. Ibid., 54.
27. Ibid., 54–57.
28. Ibid., 54.

It is no wonder that many Americans see their prime freedom in democracy not as that of participation in running their government. They have, practically speaking, no experience with that. Rather, they rejoice in what they see as their true freedom, their consumer freedom: their right to head for the stores to buy their happiness. So Washington's birthday, Lincoln's birthday, Memorial Day, Independence Day—all the patriotic holidays, and all the other holidays as well—become occasions for giant sales at the malls. Privatized democracy is symbolically reaffirmed in the ritual of holiday sale shopping. The vision of democracy as the participation of the people in the process of self-government is relegated to a secondary place in American political consciousness.

CHAPTER 4

Public Democracy

Although privatized democratic ideas have long enjoyed a privileged position in American society, the Jeffersonian tradition of public democracy has represented a constant ideological undercurrent. It has continually challenged the demobilizing tendencies of the dominant ideology, urging popular participation in a vital public sphere. The Jeffersonian tradition has been carried forward, expanded, and refined in important ways by a number of theorists, including John Dewey, C. Wright Mills, and feminist writers such as Nancy Fraser, Carol Gilligan, Carol Gould, and others. These theorists recognize many of the contradictions and shortcomings of American democratic ideology and practice. They take the participatory, publicly oriented conception of democracy as a theoretical guidepost, while noting the concrete ways in which social and political reality have diverged from it. They then propose various ways to move society back toward that goal.

An analysis of the ideas of these theorists makes it possible to create a portrait of the ideal public democratic citizen. With this picture in mind, it is possible to begin to sketch the outlines of public democratic education.

The Public: Its Importance and Its Problems

Dewey believes that communication is what holds a democratic community together. The process of people discussing their individual and group desires, needs and prospective actions, allows them to discover their shared interests in the consequences of their actions. This is what generates "social consciousness" or "general will," and creates the ability to act on collective goals. It is this process of communication and deliberation over collective goals that constitutes a democratic public.[1]

Mills agrees with this understanding of how a public should function. However, Mills envisions not a single monolithic public, but rather a society of many publics. In "a society of publics, discussion is the ascendant means of communication, and the mass media . . . simply enlarge and animate this discussion, linking one face-to-face public with the discussions of another."[2] Through public discussion, opinions are formed on social issues. When these opinions are translated into action, people exercise control of their society.[3]

Thus communication should serve two main purposes for the public. First, it provides information so that people can understand the shared social consequences of individual and group actions. Second, through discussion it allows for the formation of public opinion, which can become the basis for democratic action. In the United States today, there is an abundance of information. Yet most citizens are involved in relatively little public discussion, and even less public action. This represents a serious problem for a country that professes to be democratic.

Dewey finds the roots of this dysfunctional public in the rise of industrial capitalism. With industrialization and urbanization has come the growth of enormous corporate organizations, which dominate social life and exert a major influence on government. These large-scale organizations have become "the most significant constituents of the public and the residence of power" in society, because "they are the most potent and best organized of social forces."[4] The official public sphere for the debate of major public issues is now dominated by these organized, well-funded, and strategically

---

1. John Dewey, *The Public and Its Problems* (Chicago: Swallow Press, 1988, orig. 1927), 153–54.

2. C. Wright Mills, *Power, Politics and People*, ed. Irving Louis Horowitz, (New York: Oxford University Press, 1963), 35.

3. Ibid., 36, 355.

4. Dewey, 107–8.

positioned corporate forces. The voices (and potential influence) of ordinary citizens are simply drowned out.

In this context, privatized democratic ideology's conception of the government role as merely the protector of property interests has serious political consequences. It legitimizes government's catering to corporate needs. It works against the development of a fully inclusive democratic public which can command the service of its government for truly public ends.[5] Dewey notes the result: "the Public seems to be lost; it is certainly bewildered."[6]

Mills describes the same tendencies in American society, as they were played out some thirty years after Dewey's comments were written. Mills argues that control over society's most momentous decisions has passed into the hands of a small "power elite" made up of members of the top leadership in business, the military, and politics.[7] Beneath the power elite there is a middle level of power, populated by some members of the middle and professional classes and their interest groups, as well as professional politicians at local, state, and federal levels, including members of Congress. Members of this group are primarily concerned with locally oriented issues; and when concerned with larger issues, it is with respect to how those bear on local concerns. They rarely gain (and maintain) access to power over the broad international decisions that most strongly shape American society. These decisions rest firmly in the hands of the power elite.[8]

The third and lowest level of power is that of ordinary citizens— the general public. Mills concurs with Dewey that the public is in disarray, exerting very little influence in political affairs. But whereas Dewey sympathetically notes the public's bewilderment, Mills takes a much more cynical view: "If we accept the Greeks' definition of the idiot as an altogether private man, then we must conclude that many American citizens are now idiots."[9]

Both Dewey and Mills believe that industrialization and urbanization have undermined the possibility of building the kind of participatory democratic public that Jefferson imagined. They note the

---

5. Ibid.
6. Ibid., 114, 116.
7. Mills, *Power, Politics and People*, 26.
8. Ibid., 30–32.

concentration of power in corporations and large organizations, dwarfing the diffused power that individuals might exercise in their government. They also see a breakdown of face-to-face communication, and with it, the fading of possibilities for fully inclusive public discussion, the key to democratic deliberation and action.

The United States has become a mass society. The official public sphere, where most discussion and debate over important social decisions takes place, is now constituted by the mass media. As a result, far fewer people express opinions as hear them, and to a large extent, people have become mere media markets.[10] There is little or no opportunity for people to answer back quickly or effectively to what they hear through the mass media. In addition, channels for putting opinions into action, such as interest groups and political parties, are controlled by large organizations.[11] Most ordinary individuals have little or no influence in these organizations, even if they are members. In such a situation, people

> lose their will for decision because they do not possess the instruments for decision; they lose their sense of political belonging because they do not belong; they lose their political will because they see no way to realize it.[12]

Most people have become passive listeners and viewers, not active discussants and participants.

Of course many contemporary theorists would disagree with a characterization of people as a passive mass who accept media messages exactly as they are disseminated. In this contemporary view, the receivers of mass media messages construct the meanings of those messages through a process of "negotiation that takes place between the text and its socially situated viewers."[13]

However, it must be remembered that an important part of a viewer's social situation is the influence of society's hegemonic ideologies. We call an ideology hegemonic not only because it is the

---

9. Ibid., 24.

10. Ibid., 35.

11. Ibid., 355.

12. Ibid., 37.

13. Paolo Carpignano, Robin Andersen, Stanley Aronowitz and William DiFazio, "Chatter in the Age of Electronic Reproduction: Talk Television and the 'Public Mind,'" *Social Text* 25/26 (1990): 49.

ideology of society's dominant groups. An ideology is hegemonic precisely because most people in society accept its explanations and justifications of social reality. Therefore although readers of media texts may control the construction of meanings, they do not simply invent the materials with which to construct them. Unless there are glaring contradictions between people's lived experience and the meanings provided by the dominant ideologies, they have no reason to construct meanings that differ from those of the dominant ideologies.

In fact, even if there are glaring contradictions, hegemonic ideologies remain a powerful enough force that people often will still settle, despite their doubts, for dominant "commonsense" explanations of social reality. To take a classic example, that is why people are so often willing to accept government and media pronouncements about the righteousness and inevitability of rushing off to war. Most people patriotically support war efforts despite the obvious personal risk of life; the sometimes blatant elite commercial motives behind cries for war; not to mention questions about the morality of war, or about the consequences of expending the vast quantities of a nation's resources that are required for war.

The Persian Gulf War was a case in point. There was substantial public information that should have raised people's doubts about U.S. motives for going to war—most prominently President Bush's early public statements about the need to protect oil interests. However, official public pronouncements were then hastily reshaped to support the cause of destroying the totalitarian menace, Saddam Hussein, and "restoring" democracy to Kuwait. (This, despite the fact that Kuwait had always been patently undemocratic.) The flood of yellow ribbons and American flags onto U.S. streets provided compelling evidence that most people had accepted, at least temporarily, the dominant ideological appeals to patriotism and defense of "freedom."

This is not to deny the possibility of resistance to dominant ideologies. Clearly people all have the potential to construct their own meanings of media messages, based on their personal experience and knowledge. Yet while people have the potential to create their own meanings, they often create meanings that are very close to those that were intended by the sources of the messages; that is, they create meanings that coincide with dominant ideologies.

For most people, critical reading of mass-media messages and the political and social world around them does not come naturally. Just as students must develop the skill to read literature or legal texts critically, all citizens must develop their ability to read critically mass-media messages, as well as the social texts of the political and social forces that act upon them in their everyday lives. The fact that individuals have the potential to learn to read critically their social world and to act independently based on their reading of it, is nevertheless a very hopeful idea. That people can think and act independently of dominant ideologies and entrenched social practices raises the possibility that the privatistic tendencies of U.S. democracy can be challenged.

That is why Mills' comment about American citizens as idiots, despite its cynical charm, comes across as much too strong. By labelling American citizens idiots, that is, "altogether private" people, Mills seems to deny the possibility that people have the capability to interpret reality, discuss it, and act independently on public issues. But recognizing the potential of individuals to think critically about social reality and act to affect it is one thing; realizing that potential on a mass scale, and building democratic publics made up of people who think and act independently, is an infinitely more difficult proposition.

The Role of Education in Developing Democratic Publics

For Dewey, to constitute an inclusive democratic public, it is necessary for people to understand the processes of change in society.[14] Therefore a "science" of society is needed to conduct "social inquiry" into the social consequences of significant individual and collective actions.[15] The implication is that social scientists must play an important role in helping people understand social reality. The knowledge of social reality that social scientists produce must then be fully disseminated, in a form that is engaging and comprehensible to all. For unless the findings of social inquiry are understood, "they cannot seriously affect the thought and action of members of the public."[16] Not surprisingly, Dewey suggests that

---

14. Dewey, 165–66.
15. Ibid., 177.
16. Ibid., 183.

there must also be a related inquiry approach to education to develop ordinary people's (as opposed to just social scientists') abilities to comprehend their social world and act in it.[17] This corresponds to the idea put forth in chapter 1 about the need for proponents of public democracy to educate not only leaders and academics (organic intellectuals), but also to educate *all* citizens as intellectuals who can critically understand and take action in their social world.

Mills, too (his cynicism notwithstanding), believes that inclusive democratic publics can and must be developed. He believes that education can play a critical role in this process. Education should help people become self-educating individuals, capable of turning "personal troubles and concerns into social issues," which can then be publicly examined. The exercise of this capability is the cornerstone for the construction of democratic publics.[18] Mills feels that such an education will cultivate community leaders and other critical-thinking citizens who can mediate and interpret the information that comes through the mass media, and potentially enable them to "answer back," transforming a one-way media-to-mass communication into a public discussion.[19]

Mills believes that liberating education must be linked with, and supportive of, "movements with direct political relevance" in the larger society. Schools can nurture the kind of intellectual development and interaction which produces leaders and activists who can help social movements grow.[20] These movements become new publics in which people who have been excluded from the official public spheres can participate.

Mills' idea of promoting education that will cultivate community leaders and critical-thinking citizens linked with social movements, finds its echo in Manning Marable's ideas on building multicultural

---

17. Ibid., 201; also Dewey, *Democracy and Education* (New York: The Free Press, 1966, orig. 1916).

18. Mills, 367–68. Mills writes here on the education available in the metropolitan liberal arts college for adults, but his comments are relevant for education more generally, provided it is a liberating, publicly oriented education, of which I will speak in greater detail later. Mills, like Dewey, also believes that social scientists exercise an important responsibility in educating the general public about the connections between private troubles and public issues. See C. Wright Mills, *The Sociological Imagination* (New York: Oxford University Press, 1959), 3–24.

19. Ibid., 371.

20. Ibid., 373.

democracy. Marable calls for the creation of "Freedom Schools" for young, budding community activists. These schools would have a "curriculum which teaches young people about their own protest leaders, which reinforces their identification with our collective cultures of resistance, [and] strengthen[s] our political movements."[21]

Schools can act as incubators of citizens' democratic values, and their capacities for thinking, discussion, and debate; and they can be forums in which public discussion takes place. They can also provide an institutional setting in which people actually begin to take control of their personal and social futures. Schools can (although they generally do not) allow and encourage students to become self-directed learners. As students make both the process and content of their education their own, they enter into a process of self-discovery and self-formation. Part of this process involves coming to an understanding of the self as an agent who acts within existing social structures, affected and limited by them, but also capable of resisting and influencing them. At their best, schools will provide opportunities for students to take this journey of discovery and formation of self, in its interaction with society. They can do this through focused study of, and experiential learning in, the social world outside of school.

In these ways schools can help build publics that will develop new understandings of social reality. Discussion and debate about social reality can lead to identifying problems and their sources, developing possible solutions and working for change. If vital democratic movements exist, schools can help prepare people to participate in them. If such movements are in decline, schools can help nurture the kinds of thinking, discussion, and experience that are necessary for their renewal.[22] Schools can lay the groundwork for people to organize and act publicly.

Social Movements as Counterpublics

Historically, various political and social movements have asserted themselves in American life. Often they have been formed as

---

21. Manning Marable, "Multicultural Democracy: The Emerging Majority for Justice and Peace," in *The Crisis of Color and Democracy* (Monroe, ME: Common Courage Press, 1992), 256.

22. Mills, 369–73.

responses by subordinated social groups to domination by the larger society, and exclusion of their voices from official public spheres. Thus "women, workers, peoples of color, and gays and lesbians" have organized "subaltern counterpublics," where they can articulate new understandings of their "identities, interests and needs."[23] Nancy Fraser cites feminism as an example of such a counterpublic,

> with its variegated array of journals, bookstores, publishing companies, film and video distribution networks, lecture series, research centers, academic programs, conferences, conventions, festivals, and local meeting places. In this public sphere, feminist women have invented new terms for describing social reality, including "sexism," "the double shift, "sexual harassment," and "marital, date and acquaintance rape."[24]

Through their activities in these counterpublics, politically marginalized groups can participate in society's definition (or redefinition) of social issues, and influence decisions about actions to be taken. Their critique of accepted conceptions of social reality and its problems helps create new understandings of how society should be organized and run. By their participation in counterpublics, people challenge the anti-participatory tendencies of privatized democracy.

One important critique of American democracy comes from counterpublics which are calling for the construction of "multicultural democracy" in the United States. According to Manning Marable, multicultural democracy is a project that works to "transform the larger society, . . . restoring humanity and humanistic values to a system which is materialistic, destructive to the environment, and oppressive" to working and poor people, women, people of color, and gays and lesbians.[25]

Feminist counterpublics have also produced a comprehensive critique of American social and political ideology and practice. This critique contributes several important themes to a new vision of what is required to create a more inclusive, just and public democracy. The

---

23. Nancy Fraser, "Rethinking the Public Sphere: A Contribution to the Critique of Actually Existing Democracy," in *Social Text*, 25/26 (1990): 67.
24. Ibid.
25. Marable, 258–59.

following section discusses these themes, as they emerge in the writings of a number of contemporary feminist social theorists.[26]

Feminism's Contributions to a New Vision of Democracy

There are at least three central, related themes in feminist theory that should be integrated into any valid understanding of the essential components of a public democratic society:

1. The natural social connectedness and interdependence of individuals, and the need for an ethic of care and responsibility that corresponds to that interdependence.
2. Reconceptualizing the relationship between the private sphere and the public sphere.
3. Equality for all in terms of economic, social and political rights.

I will discuss each in turn.

1. Social Interdependence and the Need for an Ethic of Care

Liberal theory, particularly in its utilitarian individualist variety, conceives of independent, egoistic individuals as the fundamental units of society. This understanding of society makes a valuable contribution to democratic theory in its conceptualization of individual rights and freedoms. However, it also generates strong ideological pressures that work against people's ability to conceive of and carry out the ongoing public activities that are necessary for democracy.

Feminist writers have theorized alternative conceptions of society in which individuals are understood as socially constituted, interde-

---

26. Although there is a rapidly growing body of literature calling for multicultural democracy, I have found that feminist theory provides a somewhat more comprehensive critique of American democracy, and is more useful for my purposes. In any case, there is a great deal of shared theoretical ground between the two perspectives, and a number of theorists participate in both counterpublics.

pendent beings. For example, "maternal feminists" draw on the experience of women in childbearing and childrearing to portray the individual as a person grounded in relationships.[27] They propose a politics that follows from such interconnectedness, one that is based on an ethic of care and responsibility such as that which Carol Gilligan identifies with women's voice.[28]

There has been some debate among feminists over how the idea of an ethic of care should be used in feminist theories of democratic citizenship. My view is that an ethic of care and responsibility is the necessary foundation for a democratic public which serves the needs of all its members.

If one accepts that individuals are socially constituted beings, it follows that "the health of the social whole is literally vital to a socially constituted individual's well-being."[29] So there is an individualistic rationale for nurturing the society as a whole.

However, maintenance and development of the social whole requires a more communal ethic—an ethic of care and responsibility. *Care*, which is based on empathy for others, provides the moral and humanitarian impetus for people to work together to help all members of society, including those most in need, develop to their full potential. That is, it provides an ethical motive for people to work toward public goals, instead of purely individualistic or private goals. A sense of *responsibility* calls on people to take up the burden of participating in public life and working for the public good. It also serves as a check on individualistic tendencies toward socially irresponsible behavior, that may benefit a particular individual or group at the expense of the larger society. An ethic of care and responsibility provides the sense of community which is necessary for building an inclusive, democratic public life, and striving for a common good.

---

27. Mary G. Dietz, "Context Is All: Feminism and Theories of Citizenship," *Daedalus*, Fall 1987, 10–11.

28. Carol Gilligan, *In a Different Voice* (Cambridge, MA: Harvard University Press, 1982), 164.

29. Frances Moore Lappe, *Rediscovering America's Values* (New York: Ballantine Books, 1989), 13. Although Lappe is probably not known specifically as a feminist theorist, I find that her writing and activist work are infused with an ethic of care.

It must be stressed that this ethic of care cannot remain linked exclusively to the intimate relations of family life.[30] It must be projected outward toward all members of the society.

Carol Gould takes this position in elaborating her democratic theory. She argues that the fundamental units of society are "individuals-in-relations" or "social individuals."[31] By taking individuals-in-relations as a starting point, Gould makes it impossible to fall into theorizing an individualistic, privatized democracy. She builds her theory of democracy on a concept of equal positive freedom, understanding freedom as self-development. Self-development depends on the actions of individuals as agents in their own development. However, since individuals are "social beings," they must "act in and through their social relations" and social institutions. Thus "freedom . . . requires the full development of both individuality and community."[32]

Traditionally, the complementary concerns of individuality and community have not been valued equally in public life. In public democracy, the concern with community, as well as related concerns with the nurturing of life and with peace, must be assigned much greater importance.[33]

2. From "Private" Concerns to Public Issues

There are two main ways of drawing the distinction between private and public issues. The traditional way is to consider public

---

30. This is Dietz's main concern and criticism of the maternal feminists—that they have no commitment to public life; that they are apolitical. I would argue, with Joan Tronto, that an ethic of care can and indeed must be the basis for a full theory and practice of democracy. I also agree with Tronto that it expressly must not be understood as gender-based and linked to women. Dietz, 13. Joan Tronto, "Beyond Gender Difference to a Theory of Care," in *Signs* 12, 4 (1987).

31. Carol C. Gould, *Rethinking Democracy: Freedom and Social Cooperation in Politics, Economics and Society* (New York: Cambridge University Press, 1988), 105.

32. Carol C. Gould, "Private Rights and Public Virtues: Women, the Family and Democracy," in *Beyond Domination: New Perspectives on Women and Philosophy*, ed. Carol C. Gould (Totowa, NJ: Rowman and Allanheld, 1984), 5.

33. Ibid., 17. Gould also notes that such traditionally "masculine" public values as "individual achievement and self-esteem" should play a much greater role in the private sphere of personal relations.

everything relating to the law or government; and to classify as private all matters relating to "economic, cultural, personal, or family life." The second method of dividing private and public is to consider public all of institutionalized social life, including government and corporate bureaucracies and the activities connected with them. The private would then include all non-institutionalized life, such as interpersonal relations and individual actions.[34]

Historically, whichever way the private/public distinction has been drawn, it has been used to validate certain issues as worthy of public consideration. By the same token it has served to ban other issues, and the people involved in those issues, from public discussion and action. So, for example, within the first framework, the activities of individuals and corporations in the economic realm are considered private matters, in which public regulation and interference are to be minimized. Of course, the second conceptualization disputes this, putting all institutionalized social life, including economic activity, within the public realm, thereby opening it to public action.

The question of which matters are appropriate for public action continues to be fiercely debated. Indeed, the debate has intensified since the late 1970s, when conservative political forces began to solidify their strength. But in the current debate, neither of the older conceptualizations of public and private are adequate.

Starting in the late 1970s, conservatives have crusaded for privatization and deregulation of the economy and of many aspects of government activity, including public schooling.[35] At the same time, the conservative "family values" discourse has become a thinly veiled drive to weaken or ban a number of private, individual rights such as women's control over reproductive decisions, freedom of artistic expression, and freedom to choose one's sexual orientation. So on economic matters, conservatives wish to operate under the first conceptualization of public as only that which has to do with the law and government; and even working under this narrow definition, they want to shrink the public sphere by having the private

---

34. Ibid., 7.
35. Ideas for privatizing education include proposals for publicly funded vouchers for private schools, and corporate take-overs of public school systems.

sector and "markets" attempt to manage problems or tasks that the government now does. However, when it comes to issues of personal or family life, conservatives want to expand the public sphere, so that they can more readily regulate certain formerly private activities.

For very different reasons, feminists have also pushed for a broadening of the definition of public to include not only those issues that are connected with the state or with institutional life, but all issues that can be considered "of concern to everyone."[36] Feminists have noted that historically women, and many of the issues connected with women's socially defined and restricted roles as wives and mothers, have been relegated to the private sphere of domestic life.[37] This meant that under cover of their assignment to private, family life, women were excluded from full participation in public life. They also effectively lost their equal rights as individuals, since these rights could only be protected in the public sphere of law and government.

Feminists have not allowed this situation to go unchallenged. Like conservative family-value crusaders, they have fought to bring formerly "private" issues into the public sphere of debate and government policymaking. However, in stark contrast to the conservative project of bringing private issues into the public sphere in order to limit individual expression and freedom, feminists have sought to expand the public sphere in order to protect and strengthen individual rights and freedoms.

Nancy Fraser makes the argument that no issue can be excluded a priori from public discussion. There is no way to determine in advance of discussion whether an issue is indeed "private," or whether it is shared privately by a large number of people and might be linked to common causes or amenable to public solutions. She cites the example of the problem of wife or partner battering. This was traditionally considered a private, "domestic" problem, and was therefore excluded from discussion in the official public sphere. It was only when the women's movement forced the issue into public discussion and debate, as a problem that is widespread

36. Fraser, 71.
37. Ibid., 59–60.

in patriarchal societies, that it was recognized as a public issue that should be dealt with institutionally as well as privately.[38]

It is in this sense that the feminist theme "the personal is political" takes on concrete meaning. This slogan is based on the idea that what happens in personal life is connected to what happens in public, political life. In its most powerful sense, it means critically examining one's personal experience, especially one's experience of injustice or oppression, and coming to understand its connection with larger social structures and forces. The critical step is then to begin to "act politically to change and transform the world," to eliminate injustice and oppression.[39]

There are a multitude of other issues besides wife or partner battering, that could, and indeed formerly have been considered "private" concerns of individuals, of families, or of the economic marketplace. Through public discussion and debate, often initiated in counterpublics, it has been recognized that these issues can and should be addressed publicly, through social, legal, and political institutions. A few obvious examples are rape, AIDS, child care, racial and ethnic discrimination, unemployment, and all manner of workers' health, safety, and organizational rights. This process seems to be very much what C. Wright Mills had in mind when he spoke of the need to link private troubles to public issues.

There is another sense in which the feminist idea of connecting private life and public life, that is, in which the personal is political, is relevant. Since individuals are socially constituted, ongoing interpersonal relations (which are normally considered to take place in the private sphere) have an impact on people's character formation. In ongoing social contexts where interpersonal relations are based on a recognition of "the agency and the equality of others," individuals are encouraged to develop such values.[40] Values which respect

---

38. Ibid., 71. Of course, the issue of wife-battering is still often treated as a private, or "family matter." It is kept as much as possible out of the public spheres of the justice system and the mass media, and it is thereby allowed to continue. This fact was clearly demonstrated by the recent public disclosure of O. J. Simpson's long-time pattern of wife-battering, which was an open secret in Hollywood and among his media colleagues and employers (not to mention the police). It was only forced into the public view after Simpson became a suspect in his ex-wife's murder.

39. bell hooks, "Feminist Politicization: A Comment," in *Talking Back: Thinking Feminist, Thinking Black* (Boston: South End Press, 1989), 111.

40. Gould, "Private Rights and Public Virtues," 7.

other people's agency and equality are an essential foundation for a democratic character. That is why it is important that socializing institutions such as public schools encourage young people to inter-act in ways which affirm the agency and equality of others. The development of a democratic character in individuals, in turn, cre-ates a force for a democratic public life. In addition, if public life is inclusive, democratic, and egalitarian, it will reinforce such values in interpersonal relations.[41]

3. Equality

Central to feminism has been the belief in the essential equality of women and men, and the struggle to achieve for women the equal social, economic, and political rights that they should enjoy. Women's experience of domination and inequality in society has also sensi-tized feminists to the systemic inequalities that other subordinate groups face. It has imbued feminist democratic theory with an acute awareness of the need for substantive equality in social life as a precondition for democratic practice.

Feminism's first concern is with women's struggle for equality with men. Feminism demands the "recognition that women are 'individuals' like men . . . autonomous persons, free and equal . . . beings who can enter into the practice of self-assumed political obligation."[42] A prerequisite for women's autonomy is control over the childbearing function. That is, women must have access to birth control as well as safe, legal, and affordable abortion.

Furthermore, social institutions must be structured so that the care of dependent members of society (primarily children, but also the sick and the elderly) does not automatically devolve privately upon the family, and ultimately on women.[43] Society must take greater collective responsibility for care of its dependent members, so that women do not retain such responsibilities as part of their

---

41. Gould, "Private Rights and Public Virtues," 8.

42. Carole Pateman, *The Problem of Political Obligation: A Critique of Liberal Theory* (Berkeley: University of California Press, 1985), 176.

43. Johanna Brenner, "Feminist Political Discourses: Radical versus Liberal Approaches to the Feminization of Poverty and Comparable Worth," in *Women, Class and the Feminist Imagination*, ed. Karen V. Hansen and Ilene J. Philipson (Philadelphia: Temple University Press, 1990), 494.

forced gender roles. These are perhaps the most basic conditions for women's equality. Women cannot participate freely and equally in society as long as they are forced by social pressure, or by the lack of institutional alternatives, into specified gender roles.

Even if freed from the burdens of unchosen, unmanaged childbearing and dependent care, much more is required before women will enjoy full and equitable access to the benefits of social, economic and political life. The struggle to achieve women's equality has led feminist theorists to a commitment to universal social equality. For example, Johanna Brenner calls for social "interdependence and the legitimate claim of each individual on the community to meet her or his needs for good and productive work, physical sustenance, emotional support and social recognition."[44] This is similar to Gould's insistence on equality of access for all to the material and social conditions of self-development.[45]

The right to the conditions of self-development implies the right to participate in the creation and management of those conditions. This means that the arenas in which decisions are made about the creation and disposition of the conditions of individual development must be open to the participation of those who are affected by the decisions. They must become public spheres. By this definition, then, not only the political arena must be open to full democratic participation, but so also must be the economic arena.[46]

For society to be democratic, participation in these public spheres must be on an equal basis. Fraser points out that in the dominant liberal conception, existing social inequalities are assumed not to affect discussion or deliberation in the public sphere. Social inequalities are supposedly bracketed, set aside so that participants can "speak to each other as if they were social and economic peers."[47] However, in practice, social inequalities are not set aside so easily in official public spheres. Often the myth of equal participation in discussion and deliberation obscures a dynamic in which members of dominant social groups actually retain control of the process.

---

44. Ibid.
45. Gould, *Rethinking Democracy*, 25.
46. Ibid., 25–26.
47. Fraser, 63. Fraser takes Habermas' conception of the public sphere as the liberal model that she is criticizing. This conception coincides with privatized democratic ideas of the public sphere.

Participants from subordinate social groups—women, workers, the poor, and members of non-dominant racial or ethnic groups—"are silenced, encouraged to keep their wants inchoate, and heard to say 'yes' when what they have said is 'no.' "[48]

This problem is compounded by the fact that the mass media, which are the primary means for the communication of information and ideas relevant to public deliberations, are not freely accessed or controlled. They are, with a few exceptions, privately owned and run for profit, subject only to limited government regulation.[49] The media can be accessed either by paying for a message to be carried, or by decisions of news organizations or program producers that a particular event, story or piece of information will "sell." As a result, those who do not have a great deal of money to spend, or are not by their social position alone considered newsworthy, find it difficult to get their messages carried by the mainstream media.

For all of these reasons, it is clear that equal participation does not currently exist in the public spheres where issues are debated regarding the creation of the conditions necessary for people's self-development. Equal democratic participation requires a much greater degree of social equality. Of course, feminists are not the first to make this argument. Related points have been made by many democratic theorists, some of whom were discussed earlier, and by writers on multicultural democracy.

The feminist movement, movements of peoples of color, and other progressive counterpublics, not only make the theoretical argument for equality, but also struggle concretely to achieve it, so that public democratic participation can be possible. The struggle for equality goes on through complex networks of organizations, publications, cultural productions, and legal and political activities.

Summary: Contributions of Feminism to Public Democratic Theory

Feminist ideas and practices have contributed much to the creation of a new vision of U.S. democracy. Feminists have theorized the

---

48. Jane Mansbridge, "Feminism and Democracy," *The American Prospect* 1 (Spring 1990): 127, quoted in Fraser, 64.
49. Fraser, 64–65.

need for an ethic of care and responsibility—an indispensable build-ing-block for a society that intends to be publicly oriented, egalitar-ian, and democratic. They have stretched and reshaped the debate over the proper relationship between the personal and the political (the private and the public). Feminism has emphasized the need for substantive social equality as a prerequisite for equal participation in expanded and inclusive democratic public spheres. Feminism has also organized and worked to project its program of social, eco-nomic, and political transformation onto ever wider publics, and to attempt to implement it point by point.

Strengths and Limitations of Counterpublics as Vehicles for Democratic Change

The feminist movement is not the only counterpublic through which people are working to make their voices heard. As was noted earlier, similar counterpublics have been created by other subordinated groups, including African-Americans, Latinos, Native Americans, and Asians; as well as non-ethnic-based groups such as gays and lesbians, envi-ronmentalists, workers, and political activists of various persuasions. Counterpublics are born when people are driven together by the oppression of their social situation, or by some other shared sense of injustice or common cause. In a non-egalitarian, multicultural society, counterpublics can serve as arenas where subordinated groups develop and strengthen their cultural identities and identify the major obstacles that confront them.

The processes of ideological and practical change are closely in-tertwined in the work of counterpublics. Within counterpublics, participants generate the discourses that they will direct toward influencing wider publics.[50] The work of counterpublics is in this sense ideological. They produce counterhegemonic discourses which attempt to undermine and replace dominant conceptions of social reality. At the same time, these movements also work through legal,

---

50. Ibid., 67. Fraser notes that subaltern counterpublics are not necessarily democratic; and even if they intend to be democratic, they sometimes do not act openly or democratically. But to the extent that they challenge the exclusionary practices of dominant public spheres, and "help expand discursive spaces," they at least potentially contribute to building a more inclusive democracy.

political, economic, and cultural means to reshape concrete social structures and social relations. In turn, this practical work itself can have the effect of changing or reinforcing the consciousness of both participants and non-participants. An important aspect of this change process is the educational nature of much of what goes on in these groups.

Education takes place through counterpublics in a number of ways. First, the sharing of participants' personal experiences helps them recognize that their private troubles might in fact be rooted in public issues, and therefore might be amenable to public solutions. Second, an important process of dissemination and exchange of ideas and information takes place through their intricate networks. Third, a great deal of discussion and debate takes place in counterpublics. This contributes to the formation of group identities, definition of problems, examination of structures of power, and proposals for action. Fourth, participation in political actions provides invaluable experience which can further influence people's political worldviews, as well as nurture their ability to act publicly and effectively in the future. Finally, political actions and the articulation of counterhegemonic ideas also contribute to educating larger publics, outside the counterpublic.

Unfortunately, existing counterpublics are by no means currently mobilizing vast majorities of U.S. citizens for mass participation in democratic publics. So although they represent a positive social development, their existence, in itself, does not mean that widespread democratic participation is at hand. Part of the problem is that counterpublics are often seen—and often see themselves—in terms defined by privatized democracy. The work of counterpublics is therefore understood not in public, universal terms, as a struggle for full inclusion and opportunity for the self-development of all. Rather, counterpublics are sometimes understood by their members and by larger publics in particularistic terms. Operating under particularistic self-conceptions, the interaction of diverse publics can degenerate into a pluralistic struggle for the self interest of antagonistic groups. The gain of one group is understood as coming only at the expense of others.

To build public democracy, counterpublics must reject the pluralistic temptation to attempt to enhance their own group interests at the expense of others. They must work for their own concerns within a context of working toward the good of the whole society. The counterweight against the centrifugal forces of self-interested pluralism is an ethic of care and responsibility. Only such an ethic will enable multiple counterpublics to communicate across their differences. It is also crucial that they keep open the channels of communication and dialogue between themselves and the larger society. Only through dialogue can there be the possibility of mutual learning, and the creation of new and broader definitions of the public good. In this way, cross-public deliberation can lead to agreement on overall social goals, and actions to be taken to foster the self-development of *all* members of society.[51]

The Need for Ideological Change

For the members of counterpublics and others to develop an ethic of care and responsibility requires ideological change. Average citizens must be encouraged to reconceptualize their commonsense ideas about their relationship to other members of society, as well as about democracy and their role as citizens in their democracy.

Regarding their relationship to other members of society, people must come to view each other as equal, interdependent members of a social whole. They must see that they are indeed individuals, but they are individuals-in-relations. Their individuality itself is formed in the interaction of individual agency with existing social relations and social structures. Society provides the context within which individuals exercise their freedom of self-development.

Society is an individual's home. If there are weaknesses in society, if some individuals or groups are not able to develop to their full potential, they cannot be full participants and contributors to society. As a result, the social context in which all members of society seek their own development is weakened. Every individual's self-development is therefore connected to the self-development of all others in society.

The privatized and individualistic ideologies that currently dominate people's understandings of the world deny and disguise the reality of people's interdependence. These ideologies encourage

51. Ibid., 69–70.

individuals intentionally to close their eyes to the social consequences of their actions or their inaction. They replace conscious individual responsibility for shaping society, with blind faith in an economistic invisible hand. This produces the oft-repeated sentiment that market forces will solve all of society's problems. These privatistic ideologies deny that people can consciously shape their own social future. They deny in principle that people can rule themselves.

Current hegemonic understandings and practices of democracy are incapable of producing a public democracy in which people consciously shape their society's future. Privately oriented, individualistic, and consumerist understandings of democracy must be replaced with more publicly oriented, participatory democratic ideas and practices. American citizenship must be reconstructed on a foundation of public democratic values, attributes, and practices, if a public democracy is to be forged in the United States.

Characteristics of Public Democratic Citizenship

This chapter has drawn upon a wide range of social and political theorists to sketch the outlines of an alternative hegemonic vision and practice of democratic citizenship. This alternative understanding of democratic citizenship builds upon a long tradition of American political philosophy that sees democracy as publicly oriented rule by participation, as opposed to individualistic, privately oriented rule by consent. Based on this chapter's presentation of the theoretical foundations of public democracy, it is possible to develop an outline of the values, attributes, and capacities an ideal-typical American citizen would have to possess in order to participate meaningfully in a public democracy.

There are five major orienting values and attributes that public democratic citizens must share, including a number of abilities and skills people need to possess in order to participate effectively in a public democracy. Table 4.1 summarizes these key values, attributes, and capacities necessary for public democratic citizenship. Each is then discussed in turn.[52]

---

52. Footnotes will be used to help readers connect the specified public citizenship values, attributes, and capacities with some of the theorists whose work suggests them. Most of these theorists have been discussed in this or earlier chapters.

Table 4.1
Values, Attributes, and Capacities Needed
for Public Democratic Citizenship

1. An ethic of care and responsibility as a foundation for community and public life
   (a) Understanding of the interdependence of people as "individuals-in-relations"
   (b) Understanding of the need for individuals to live as responsible members of communities
2. Respect for the equal right of everyone to the conditions necessary for their self-development
   (a) A sense of justice based on that right
   (b) Principles of equal individual civil and political rights, and equal political power and voice, within a context which balances the rights of individuals against their responsibilities to the larger community
   (c) Acceptance of the fundamental equality of members of all social groups in society, including that of social groups other than one's own
       1) Acceptance of a person or a group's right to be different from oneself, or from accepted norms and values of the community, as long as the rights of others aren't threatened
3. Appreciation of the importance of the public
   (a) Appreciating need to participate in public discussion and debate, and to take action to address public issues
   (b) Recognizing need to expand and create new public spheres as sites for discussion and debate of public issues
   (c) Understanding public nature of certain personal problems
4. A critical/analytical social outlook
   (a) Habits of examining critically the nature of social reality, including the "commonsense" realities of everyday life
   (b) Habits of examining underlying relations of power in any given social situation.
5. The *capacities* necessary for public democratic participation
   (a) Analysis of written, spoken and image language
   (b) Clear oral and written expression of one's ideas
   (c) Habits of active listening as a key to communication
   (d) Facility in working collaboratively with others
   (e) Knowledge of constitutional rights and political processes
   (f) Knowledge of complexities and interconnections of major public issues to each other and to issues in the past
   (g) Self-confidence, self-reliance, and ability to act independently (within context of community)
   (h) Ability to learn more about any issue that arises

1. An ethic of care and responsibility as a foundation for community and public life.[53] This includes an understanding of the interconnectedness and interdependence of people as "individuals-in-relations"; and following from that, the need for individuals to live as responsible members of communities.[54]

2. Respect for the equal right of everyone to the conditions necessary for their self-development as individuals-in-relations.[55] This provides the basis for such fundamental liberal democratic principles as equal individual civil and political rights, and equal political power and voice. Yet it places these principles squarely within the context of a publicly oriented concept of democracy, in which the rights of individuals are balanced by their responsibilities to each other and to the larger community. A respect for equal individual rights within this context creates the possibility for a sophisticated sense of justice that continually weighs individual claims against social concerns.

Respect for everyone's equal rights to self-development involves acceptance of the fundamental equality of members of all social groups in society, including that of social groups other than one's own. This implies acceptance of a person or a group's right to be different from oneself, or from the accepted norms and values of the community, as long as that difference doesn't interfere with the rights of other community members. This acceptance and respect for difference is an essential condition for building public democracy in a multiracial, multicultural society.

3. An appreciation of the importance of the public.[56] This has several aspects, including recognizing the need to expand and create new public spheres as sites for discussion and debate of public issues; understanding the public nature of certain "personal" problems; appreciating the need to participate in public discussion and debate, and to take action to address public issues.

---

53. M. Belenky, B. Clinchy, N. Goldberger, and J. Tarule, *Women's Ways of Knowing: The Development of Self, Voice and Mind* (New York: Cambridge University Press, 1988), 228; Gilligan, 164; Tronto.

54. Gould, *Rethinking Democracy*, 105.

55. Ibid., 110.

56. Dewey, *The Public and Its Problems*, 107–16, 153–54; Mills, *Power, Politics and People*, 24–37; Mills, *The Sociological Imagination*, 3–24; Fraser, "Rethinking the Public Sphere," 56–80.

4. *A critical/analytical social outlook.*[57] A critical social outlook is geared toward examining critically the nature of social reality, including the "commonsense" realities of everyday life. It also seeks to understand the underlying relations of power in any given social situation.

5. *The capacities necessary for public democratic participation.* These capacities include analysis of written, spoken, and image language;[58] clear oral and written expression of one's ideas;[59] habits of active listening as a key to communication;[60] and facility in working collaboratively with others.[61] In addition, capacities for public participation include some knowledge of key U.S. constitutional rights, and the political processes of government, from the local to the national level. It is also necessary for public citizens to understand some of the complexities and interconnections of major public issues to each other and to issues in the past;[62] and more importantly, to know how to learn more about any important issue or set of issues that arises.[63] Finally, a public citizen must possess the self-confidence and independence of mind to be able to take appropriate public action when necessary.[64]

Table 4.1's description of the principal characteristics of the ideal public democratic citizen serves as a compass to orient the work of educators who wish to teach for public democracy. Democratic educators must begin to organize schools to teach these essential public democratic citizenship values and skills to young people.

The following chapter builds a rationale for studying existing experiments in urban democratic education. It also develops a set of ideal organizational, curricular, and pedagogical features that can be used as a tool for analyzing the work of schools which aspire to democratic education.

---

57. Mills, *Power, Politics and People*, 367–73; Giroux, *Schooling and the Struggle for a Public Life*, 155–61.

58. Mills, *Power, Politics and People*, 371; Stuart Ewen, lecture, the City University of New York Graduate Center, 9 May 1991. Ewen contends that images in mass culture are "a prime way ideas get expressed in our society." Control of images constitutes "a form of power." Consequently, the ability to analyze images is also an important form of power.

59. Mills, *Power, Politics and People*, 371.

60. M. F. Belenky, B. Clinchy, N. Goldberger, and J. Tarule, *Women's Ways of Knowing* (New York: Basic Books, 1986), 221.

61. Belenky et al.; Fraser, 76.

62. Dewey, *The Public and Its Problems*, 165–66; Jefferson, *Notes on Virginia*, 148.

63. Dewey, *The Public and Its Problems*, 201; Dewey, *Democracy and Education* (New York: The Free Press, 1966, orig. 1916).

64. Mills, *Power, Politics and People*, 367–71.

CHAPTER 5

Education for Public
Democratic Citizenship

Transforming American Democracy through Education

At least since the time of Thomas Jefferson, American education has been seen as a means for preparing young people for democratic citizenship. Schools have long been sites for the "socialization" of students according to dominant notions of privately oriented democratic citizenship. However, a number of critical educational theorists have argued that schools can play an important role in promoting alternative understandings of democracy, and can thereby help build a more democratic and just society.[1] Indeed, schools have always been sites in which relatively small numbers of progressive and radical democratic educators have prepared young people for active, critical, publicly oriented citizenship. There is great potential for more such work to be done in schools.

For activist researchers or educators who wish to build a movement for public democracy, the question becomes, simply: *How can*

---

1. To name just a few: Michael Apple, *Ideology and Curriculum* (New York: Routledge and Kegan Paul, 1979); Aronowitz and Giroux, *Education under Siege* and *Postmodern Education*; Giroux, *Schooling and the Struggle for Public Life*; Jesse Goodman, *Elementary Schooling for Critical Democracy* (Albany: SUNY Press, 1992); Peter McLaren, *Life in Schools* (New York: Longman, 1989); Ira Shor, *Critical Teaching and Everyday Life* (Boston: South End Press, 1980); Kathleen Weiler, *Women Teaching for Change* (South Hadley, MA: Bergin and Garvey, 1988).

83

schools be organized and run to prepare young people for public democratic citizenship? Part of the answer lies in learning from the experience of schools that are attempting to teach for public democratic citizenship. There is a need for case study research on existing schools, and individual classrooms, that are potential models of education for public citizenship. The research must examine and critique the actual workings of such schools and classrooms, so that they might be improved as educational models.

Need for Models of Democratic Urban Education

It is especially critical to hold up models of democratic education that serve inner-city populations, that is, students who are primarily of African-American, Latino, and Asian backgrounds. These students are often ill-served by their schools. This point is made by Michelle Fine, discussing high school dropout rates.

> Dropout rates nationally fall at 25 percent. In many urban high schools, however, they reach 60 and 70 percent. Dropping out of high school is, in some schools, a nearly anomalous event. In other schools, it is a shared tradition. The latter schools are low income, urban and often, "of color," and in these communities, the consequences are almost always devastating.[2]

Public democratic education would seek to break this social trap. It would teach urban students the key values and capacities they would need to be effective public democratic citizens. This would help young people of color and others take control of their lives, and work with others to accomplish personal as well as collective goals in their social, economic, and political lives. Existing models of this type of education must be identified, studied, improved upon and publicized, so that democratic urban educational reform can take place on a broader scale.

But before entering into a discussion and analysis of potential models of democratic urban public education, it is necessary to address two important prior issues: (1) What is the nature of the interaction

---

2. Michelle Fine, *Framing Dropouts*, (Albany: SUNY Press, 1991), 21.

between schools and students, as schools try to "teach" citizenship to young people? That is, what is the nature of the process of "political socialization" in schools? (2) How can researchers and democratic educational activists best study existing models of democratic schooling, and analyze what they see in such schools?

Political Socialization in Schools

Many of the important early studies of political socialization suffer from a crucial conceptual weakness. They understand socialization as a *one-directional process* in which young people are inculcated in the political values and norms of a society, to ensure the political system's persistence.[3]

R. W. Connell challenges this understanding of political socialization for failing to recognize "the conscious creative activity of the children themselves in the development of their own beliefs."[4] With this theoretical shift, Connell introduces the possibility of students as active subjects in the socialization process. William Wentworth carries the argument further by developing a theory of socialization that posits a "cultural context of interaction" which limits, but does not determine individual activity. Thus the success of the process of socialization is "directly dependent upon the willingness of the novice to submit . . . to expected conduct." Socialization in schools is therefore a negotiated process.[5]

Qualitative Studies of Democratic Schools

The focus on socialization as process and on students as agents seems to lead away from the macro-sociological and survey orientations of

---

3. Herbert Hyman, *Political Socialization* (Glencoe: The Free Press, 1959); Fred Greenstein, *Children and Politics* (New Haven: Yale University Press, 1965); Robert Hess and Judith Torney, *The Development of Political Attitudes in Children* (Garden City, NY: Doubleday, 1968).

4. R. W. Connell, *The Child's Construction of Politics* (Carlton, Australia: Melbourne University Press, 1971), 232.

5. William Wentworth, *Context and Understanding.* (New York: Elsevier, 1980), 108, 134.

the early political socialization studies.[6] It points instead to the need for micro-focused, qualitative research methods such as open-ended interviews and educational ethnography. These are some of the best techniques for gaining insight into the structures and processes of democratic schooling, and students' responses to their educational experience in democratic schools.

However, ethnographies and other qualitative studies of democratic schools cannot be interpreted in a social and political vacuum. Researchers must have a way of interpreting the qualitative data from such studies, to take into account ongoing struggles between competing visions of democracy. Researchers and educators working for public democracy need to ground themselves in a clear conception of public democratic citizenship, such as that outlined in the previous chapter. It is then possible to create a framework of analysis made up of school organizational features and practices that are most likely to engage students and encourage their development as public democratic citizens.

There is no single educational theorist who addresses adequately the kinds of school practices that will most effectively develop publicly oriented democratic worldviews and practices in young people. However, ideas drawn from a number of sources contribute to a composite picture of an "ideal-typical" secondary school designed to help prepare young people for public democratic citizenship. This "ideal-typical" model of democratic schooling will be used in Part II of this book, as a standard against which to compare and analyze two existing urban alternative public high schools, both of which consider preparing students for democratic citizenship an important part of their mission.[7]

Ideal Organization and Practices for Engaging Students and Promoting Public Democratic Citizenship

In the negotiation that takes place between the educational intentions of a school, and students' own intentions, little learning can

6. Stuart Palonsky, "Political Socialization in Elementary Schools," *The Elementary School Journal* 87.5 (1987).

7. The usefulness of ideal types in research is discussed in Max Weber, *Economy and Society*, ed. Guenther Roth and Claus Wittich (Berkeley, CA: University of California Press, 1978), 20–22.

Table 5.1
Characteristics of School Life Likely to Engage
Students in a School's Programs

1. An atmosphere in which students feel a sense of belonging or membership in the school community
2. A feeling of students' safety, both physical and emotional/psychological
3. Schoolwork with intrinsic interest for students
4. Schoolwork that is meaningful not only for school purposes, but also in the real world outside school
5. A sense of student ownership of their school

take place unless, at some level, students assent to the process. Thus even if a school takes seriously the task of preparing students for democratic citizenship, and designs its programs around this goal, it will have little success unless students are fully engaged in the schools' educational program. Moreover, the qualities necessary for publicly oriented democratic citizenship are not acquired through abstract study alone. They are acquired and honed through concrete experience as well as study. Therefore, if schools are to help develop young people's capacities for public democratic activity, they must not only teach about democratic values, but also create regular opportunities for students to develop them and use them. Democratic education must be organized and practiced in ways that involve students actively in academic work and school life.

School Characteristics that Engage Students

There are several characteristics of school life that are likely to engage students in a school's programs.[8] Some of these characteristics not only help engage students in their schoolwork, but also contribute in themselves to promoting democratic perspectives and capacities in students. The most important school characteristics for promoting student engagement are discussed below. They are also listed in summary form in table 5.1.

---

8. I draw here on Fred Newmann's important work on student engagement. Although Newmann is interested in student engagement in academic work generally, the organizational

1. Schools should create an atmosphere in which students feel a sense of belonging or membership in the school community. Students should feel welcomed and cared about, and consider themselves involved in the life of the school, not just academically, but also socially (have good friends there, participate in extracurricular and after-school activities, etc).

2. Schools should make sure that students are safe, not only physically, but also emotionally/psychologically. That is, it should be safe for students to express themselves, in and out of class; to risk making mistakes without fear of humiliation; to be open to new experiences, etc.

3. Schoolwork should have intrinsic interest for students. It should build on their prior knowledge and respond to their interests.

4. Schoolwork should be meaningful not only within the school and for school purposes, but also in the real world outside school. It should make meaningful connections to people, places, things, events, and phenomena in the real world and in history.

5. Schools should create conditions that give students a sense of ownership of them. For example, they should have some input into decisions governing their lives in the school. Students should also be allowed flexibility in how they approach their learning and at what pace they proceed. They should have the opportunity to explore questions and topics that they consider important. They should be encouraged to construct and express their growing knowledge in their own language, rather than regurgitating book language or teacher language.

---

principles he suggests for schools are also applicable to the task of engaging students in schoolwork and experiences that specifically promote democratic thinking and action. Newmann's three main categories and numerous subcategories of factors that influence student engagement have been adapted in a way which hopefully simplifies them and yet still captures their most important features. For explanations of Newmann's more detailed model of factors affecting student engagement, see Fred Newmann, "Student Engagement in Academic Work: Expanding the Perspective on Secondary School Effectiveness," in *Rethinking Effective Schools*, ed. J. Bliss and W. Firestone (Englewood Cliffs, NJ: Prentice Hall, 1991); and F. Newmann, G. Wehlage, and S. Lamborn, "Significance and Sources of Student Engagement," in *Student Engagement and Achievement in American Secondary Schools*, ed. F. Newmann (New York: Teachers College Press, 1992.)

To create education for public democracy, it is necessary, but obviously not sufficient, to engage students in their academic work. The content of the work students do, as well as the way it is organized, must be designed to help students begin to think and act democratically.

Public Democratic School Practices

An ideal-typical secondary school can do a number of things to nurture democratic qualities in young citizens. The practices that will be suggested here are, like all school practices, complex social processes. They involve a number of social actors—teachers, administrators, students, parents, other community members—with various and often changing agendas. These actors operate within a structure that is shaped by numerous and often contradictory institutional, cultural, and historical forces such as national, state, and local government and politics; the economic context; local school board policies, traditional school practices, and so on. For this reason, the practices described here are likely to have multiple, overlapping effects. Each practice nevertheless attempts to contribute to the development of one or more of the specific public citizenship values, attributes and capacities outlined in table 4.1. There are at least five key school practices for nurturing public democtratic values and attributes in high school students. These are listed in Table 5.2.

Table 5.2
School Practices for Nurturing
Public Democratic Values and Attributes

1. Creating opportunities for students to explore their interdependence with others and with nature.
2. Encouraging study of issues of equality and social justice.
3. Encouraging discussion, debate, and action on public issues.
4. Encouraging students to examine and evaluate critically the social reality in which they live.
5. Developing students' capacities for public democratic participation.

1. Exploring Students' Interdependence with Others

Schools can create opportunities for students to explore their interdependence with others, both through study and through experiential learning. One example is the study, through research and discussion, of the connections between people's actions and their effects on others and on the society as a whole. This can begin with an examination of students' own individual actions, such as their treatment of each other and of shared school facilities (classrooms, desks, bathrooms and other public spaces, etc.) and the impact this has on the quality of school life for students and staff. An examination of students' and teachers' interdependence in school life can provide a good starting point for developing an ethic of care and responsibility.

Discussion of the shared use of public facilities and public space can also be connected to such issues as the overall quality of school facilities and equipment; and levels of funding in rich versus poor communities, and white communities versus communities of color. This can lead to discussion of the need for equal rights of all community members to the conditions needed for their self-development.

Another way to explore the idea of interdependence is to do an ecological/sociological life-cycle study of common products that a society uses. This would include examining the processes of production, distribution, use and disposal of a product, and the social relations that surround each stage in the life cycle. Such a study shows some of the connections between people as consumers, users and disposers of products, and people as designers, manufacturing workers, distributors, retailers, refuse carters, and so on, of those same products. As the working conditions, standard of living, and life style of people are uncovered at various intersections with the life cycle of a product, hierarchical patterns based on class, race, and gender begin to become apparent. Such a study also gets into some of the effects on the environment of each stage of a product's life cycle. It provides initial insights into the complex interdependence of people with each other and with the earth.[9]

School practices that explore people's interdependence with others are aimed directly at developing an ethic of care and responsibil-

---

9. Ira Shor offers an excellent description of his use of a similar teaching practice, getting his students to "extraordinarily re-experience the ordinary," by doing extended social analysis of such common items as chairs and hamburgers. Ira Shor, *Critical Teaching and Everyday Life*, 156–66.

ity in young people. At the same time, they also help students develop other values and capacities that are important for public democratic citizenship. For example, study of the consequences of students' and other people's actions in school and in larger communities, along with studies of the social relations surrounding the life cycles of products can help students begin to comprehend the complexities of and connections among public issues. In addition, they help students begin to look more critically at social realities that are normally taken for granted. They also raise young people's awareness of some of the public consequences of private actions, an important step in understanding the nature of the public.

The Study of Community: Individual Rights and Responsibilities in Communities.   Another approach to exploring people's interdependence is the study of the concept of community, including analysis of what defines a community; discussion of why communities are important; analysis of the common problems and shared experiences of historical and contemporary communities; examination of students' own communities; and discussion of solutions or possible solutions to community problems. Exploration of the concept of community provides another opening for students to begin to develop an ethic of care and responsibility.

But the concept of community cannot be explored without also examining the roles of individuals in communities. This question can move students into the issue of the rights and responsibilities of individuals within various kinds of communities, including large, multicultural, would-be democratic societies such as our own.

Students can get a taste of the relationship between the rights of individuals and their responsibilities to each other and to their communities by participating in school-sponsored internships or community service work with local social service, development, or community-organizing programs. An important criterion for selecting host organizations for student placements should be that their work involves helping people secure access to the conditions necessary for self-development.[10] Thus host organizations could be service or advocacy groups dedicated to securing basic human needs

---

10. Harry Boyte discusses the limitations of many student community-service programs that are more oriented toward building students' résumés than getting them involved in addressing the needs of the community. He also describes programs that avoid this pitfall. Harry C. Boyte, "Turning On Youth to Politics," *The Nation* 252 (13 May 1991): 626–28.

such as housing, food, clothing, employment, education, health care, and so forth. Or they could be activist organizations, perhaps working within larger counterpublics to help people secure their fundamental civil and political rights.

Working with such organizations can potentially provide students with a fuller understanding of the essential relationship between individual rights and the continuing responsibility to work with others to enhance the life of the community as a whole. However, the mere fact of students' participation in community-service projects will not necessarily lead to students' development of public democratic consciousness. To be effective tools for building students' public citizenship values and skills, community-service programs should be connected to regular seminar-style meetings that provide students with opportunities to read, write, discuss, and reflect upon their experiences, as well as on the larger social and political contexts of their experiences.[11]

When participation in community service is combined with systematic reflection, it can help students develop an ethic of care and responsibility; help students become more aware of public problems and issues; allow them to experience the value of publicly oriented work; and contribute to their appreciation of the importance of public life and public action.

2. Studying Issues of Equality and Social Justice

The exploration of people's rights and responsibilities in communities can lead to investigations of the struggle for equal rights of various non-dominant social groups such as women, workers, gays and lesbians, African-Americans, Latinos, Asian-Americans, and other immigrant groups. An important part of such studies is an examination of the role of conflict in popular struggles for social justice.

---

11. Mara Gross makes a similar suggestion in her dissertation on the experiences of students in a community-service program. Gross suggests the need to make community service a central part of the curriculum, fully integrated with the students' academic work, to encourage students to process and reflect upon their community-service experiences. Mara Gross, "Reflection in Action: A Practitioner's Study of Four High School Students' Experience in Community Service" (Ed.D. diss., Teachers College, Columbia University, 1991), 188–92.

Students need to understand that social conflict and struggle are a constant part of American history, and that history is, in fact, made through struggle. A key feature of social struggle in the United States has been majority-group intolerance and economic exploitation of new immigrants and other minority groups.[12] Students should study this history in order to understand racism, how racism has served dominant social groups, and the ways in which people have organized to challenge it. Such an approach provides students with important insights into the nature of power, as well as possible models for their own attempts to work toward greater social and political power.[13]

The study of social justice movements contributes to students' understanding that American society has historically denied many social groups equal rights to the conditions they need to develop themselves to their full human potential (i.e., political rights; decent jobs with living wages and safe working conditions; good, affordable housing; quality education, etc.). It also teaches the power of organized resistance and struggle for equal rights. Finally, it highlights the need to continue to struggle for equal rights for the self-development of all members of society.

Students can also be encouraged to make connections between their own experience and the experience of the social groups they study. They can identify similar obstacles to self-development in their own lives and their own communities, and begin to recognize the public nature of certain problems which they previously may have thought of as purely "personal" or "private" problems. This can lead students to consider the nature of the public and the importance of participating in public life.

Study of Cultural Diversity.   Another approach to the study of equality and social justice issues is to encourage examination of cultural diversity in students' own school, local, and national communities. Schools should make a point of having students explore

---

12. See Ronald Takaki, *A Different Mirror: A History of Multicultural America* (New York: Little, Brown, 1993). Also see the excellent video and curriculum materials connected with *The Shadow of Hate: A History of Intolerance in America* (Montgomery, AL: Teaching Tolerance, The Southern Poverty Law Center, 1995), video and teaching materials.

13. Michael Apple, *Ideology and Curriculum*, 82–104.

and value their own cultural heritages. This type of work is important for all students, but it can be especially powerful for students of color. A prominent argument in the literature on the education of students of color, states that the legitimation and celebration of students' cultural identities contributes to their development of a strong self-image, as well as to their academic achievement.[14] Increased self-confidence and intellectual development are important prerequisites for students' social and political empowerment.

To promote the kind of cross-cultural understanding and respect that is necessary for democracy in a multicultural society, schools should have students share their knowledge of their diverse cultural heritages with each other. There should also be regular opportunities for students to discuss racial and ethnic conflict and tension in their own lives, and strategies for dealing with them. Perhaps even more important, students should be encouraged to work on cooperative projects in culturally diverse groups on a regular basis, so that intercultural tolerance and understanding will develop naturally along with the camaraderie that comes from working together for common goals.[15]

Activities that promote cross-cultural understanding and respect contribute directly to students' development of an ethic of care and responsibility. Student discussion and study of racial and ethnic tension in their experience and in their communities, along with discussion of ways to address it, are also important for developing an ethic of care and responsibility. Such discussions, in combination with the concrete experience of working on cooperative projects in mixed racial and ethnic groups, help build students' awareness of, and respect for each other's equal rights in society. School practices that value students' cultural heritages, nurture their positive self-images and facilitate their intellectual development, as well as activities that involve students in cooperative group work, are all important for students' development of the capacities necessary for public participation.

---

14. Jim Cummins, "Empowering Minority Students: A Framework for Intervention," *Harvard Education Review* 56 (February 1986): 23.

15. Daniel Goleman, "Psychologists Find Ways to Break Racism's Hold," *New York Times*, 5 September 1989, C1.

3. Discussion and Action on Public Issues.

Any of the projects discussed in the previous two sections can be conducted as collaborative group research projects. In group research projects, students work cooperatively with their peers to reach agreement on goals and strategies appropriate to their tasks, and then work to accomplish them. Traditional school practice has discouraged collaborative work, often equating it with cheating, and prohibiting it. Instead, schools have encouraged students to work as individuals in competition with each other. Yet public life requires that individuals work with others to define and act on common goals. Cooperative group research projects teach young people through experience the value and the social skills involved in working with others to achieve common goals.

Whenever possible, collaborative research projects can be action projects, linked to real issues. They can be oriented toward studying and acting on the social reality of the school itself, the surrounding community, or the larger world.

An example of an action project focused on the world outside of school might involve students doing research on a local environmental issue such as pollution of a local stream. Their work could culminate in an expose, made available for the local news media, about the type and sources of the pollution, which could be used as part of organizing efforts to pressure polluters to clean up.[16]

Action research projects give students invaluable experience in wrestling with the obstacles that come up in working with others to define public problems, locate sources of the problems, and confront

---

16. Other examples of community action research projects conducted by students and teachers are detailed in a social studies curriculum published by Educators for Social Responsibility. Case histories are provided on student campaigns to save a local forest from development by having the county government purchase it as parkland; and a petition drive to organize high school students nationally to support a nuclear weapons freeze. Educators for Social Responsibility, *Making History. A Social Studies Curriculum in the Participation Series* (Cambridge, MA: Boston Area Educators for Social Responsibility, 1984), 46–53, 55–72.

Some of the work of teachers and students using the Foxfire Approach takes on similar action research orientations. Examples of this work are chronicled in *Hands On: A Journal for Teachers* (Rabun Gap, GA: The Foxfire Fund, Inc.).

Another excellent source of articles on class research projects that have led to social action is: B. Bigelow, L. Christensen, S. Karp, B. Miner, and B. Peterson, eds., *Rethinking Our Classrooms: Teaching for Equity and Justice* (Milwaukee, WI: Rethinking Schools Limited, 1994).

the power structures that allow the problems to exist. Through these projects students learn how to do research on any issue they wish to investigate, and then how to take action on that issue. Through action research activities, young people can develop the worldviews, knowledge, and capacities they need to act publicly to help shape their social and political worlds.

4. Critical Examination of Social Reality

Schools can also encourage students to examine and evaluate critically the social reality in which they live. The most fruitful way to begin this process is through inquiry learning, which puts students in the role of inquirers, or researchers, rather than passive recipients of knowledge from teachers and textbooks.

It is especially important for students to address their critical inquiry toward uncovering the power relations inherent in existing social structures, institutions, and even in the "commonsense" relations of everyday life. Students can begin their inquiries by examining their own life experiences. They can be asked to recall situations of injustice they have either experienced or witnessed. They can then work together to analyze the social causes and power relations involved in those situations, how they responded to them, and other ways they might intervene to challenge injustice in similar situations in the future.[17]

Another part of the critical study of social reality is the study of culture. As discussed in the first chapter, cultural production plays crucial roles in both reinforcing and challenging the hegemony of existing social relations. Through a critical study of culture, students can become more conscious of the ways in which music, art, video, television, movies, advertising, and the news media support or challenge the social inequalities and unequal power relations in society.[18]

---

17. Linda Christensen, an English teacher at Jefferson High School in Portland, Oregon, uses this approach as one step in the process of getting her students to begin to look critically at the world. Linda Christensen, presentation at Rethinking Our Classrooms Institute, Portland, OR, 1 August 1994, sponsored by Network of Educators on the Americas (NECA).

18. An example of a class project in critical inquiry into popular culture (fairy tales and films) is described in Linda Christensen, "Unlearning the Myths that Bind Us," in *Rethinking Our Classrooms: Teaching for Equity and Justice*, 8–13.

Critically analyzing the social world is a crucial skill for public citizenship. Helping young people develop this skill, and the habit of employing it, is an essential charge of schools for public democracy.

5. Developing Students' Capacities for Public Democratic Participation

Analysis and Public Expression.   If students are to investigate, discuss, and debate the nature of social reality to prepare them for public democratic activity, they must develop and train a number of critical capacities. For example, they must learn to analyze written, spoken, and image language, from mass-media sources as well as face-to-face sources. People are bombarded in all their waking hours with verbal and image language intended to inform, direct, entertain, and especially to persuade them to believe or accept some idea, to act a certain way, or to buy a particular product or service. They must learn to analyze such messages to trace their source, their purpose, and what would be the consequences—that is, who would be likely to benefit or suffer—if one reacted to the messages in specific ways or not at all. This is necessary so that people can comprehend public discussion and debate, and draw their own conclusions about the concrete social significance of the various issues under discussion, and options for action on those issues.

Close textual analysis of written, spoken, and image language can only be learned through practice. Schools can offer students the intellectual support and guidance to master the craft. In *Lives on the Boundary*, Mike Rose emphasizes the importance of the guidance he received from his college mentors as he learned close reading of written texts:

> I developed the ability to read closely, to persevere in the face of uncertainty and ask questions of what I was reading. . . . My teachers modeled critical inquiry and linguistic precision and grace, and they provided various cognitive maps for philosophy and history and literature.[19]

---

19. Mike Rose, *Lives on the Boundary* (New York: Penguin Books, 1990), 58.

Schools must not only train young people in the ability to analyze various texts. They must also help students develop their capacities for expressing their ideas. Young citizens must learn to express themselves well in writing and speech. They must also learn how to get access to public forums in which to express their ideas and opinions.

Students best learn to express themselves in writing and speech by writing and speaking on meaningful subjects to real audiences. Whole language teachers seek to structure activities so that "when students talk, read, and write, they do so for some *communicative function.*"[20] Democratic educators must do the same. They should structure projects in which students communicate with real audiences as they express themselves on issues that are important to them. This could involve students gaining access to coverage in the mass media through demonstrations or other events, or even producing and distributing their own media creations such as videos, films, dramatizations, newsletters, and pamphlets. The capacity to communicate and the ability to gain access to public forums are both necessary for participation in public discussion and debate.

Knowledge of Constitutional Rights and Processes of Government. Young citizens in the United States must also possess knowledge of basic Constitutional issues and rights, and understand political processes at the local, state, and national levels. If they are to participate in the political system, they must have some sense of how it works and what their rights are. Students best learn about constitutional issues and political processes through active learning projects. Such projects can take a variety of forms. For example, students can research and perform historical role plays about important constitutional rights clashes. Or they can do action research projects which involve them in real-life political processes, such as those described earlier. What is important is that students need to become actively engaged in learning about American political rights and processes.

Active Listening and Collaborative Work.   Another capacity that is crucial for young citizens to develop, and one that is often over-

---

20. Center for the Expansion of Language and Thinking (CELT), "Some Key Principles of a Whole Language Perspective on Learning and Teaching" (Tempe, AZ: CELT, 1991).

looked, is that of active listening. In all classroom interactions, whether in discussion of students' understandings of new knowledge or their positions on social issues, students and teachers should focus first on listening, on trying to understand and empathize with the points of view that others are expressing. Disagreements can and should be voiced; but not before students and teachers have done their best to understand fully the points that are being made and where they are coming from in terms of the speaker's experience and knowledge. This helps create a classroom environment in which students "can nurture each others' thoughts to maturity."[21] Such an educational environment contrasts sharply with the more common "banking" or "adversarial" models of education.[22]

Interacting in this way allows students and teachers to learn from each other's different experiences and perspectives. It forms a foundation for effective work in collaborative groups. It also fosters patterns of communication that are in keeping with an ethic of care. Such patterns of communication are necessary for enabling democratic public spheres to function in a way that can produce agreement on public goals and strategies for achieving them.

This approach to education has much in common with what Paulo Freire calls problem-posing, dialogic education. Dialogic education creates a new relationship among students and between students and teachers.

> Through dialogue, the teacher-of-the-students and the students-of-the-teacher cease to exist and a new term emerges: teacher-student with students-teachers. The teacher is no longer merely the-one-who-teaches but one who is himself taught in dialogue with the students, who in turn while being taught also teach. They become jointly responsible for a process in which all grow. In this process, arguments based on "authority" are no

---

21. M. F. Belenky et al., 221.

22. The "banking" model of education is described in Paulo Freire, *Pedagogy of the Oppressed* (New York: Continuum, 1981), 57–74. It involves a teacher as the knowledge authority "depositing" knowledge into the "empty" heads of passive students. In the "adversarial, doubting model," teachers, and presumably students, challenge fellow students' ideas, trying to induce doubt, and from doubt, thought and learning. But since many women, as well as many students of color are already self-doubters, this model may simply discourage them from ever gaining the confidence to think for themselves. Belenky et al., 228.

longer valid; in order to function, authority must be on the side of freedom, not against it.[23]

Understanding Complexities of and Connections among Issues. In addition to developing these capacities of analysis, expression, and active listening, students must also increase their knowledge of the complexities of major public issues. To this end, schools should encourage students to investigate the linkages among issues across academic disciplines, and across national and cultural boundaries. We live in an era of global connection and interdependence in everything from capital, labor, consumer, and currency markets, to the consequences of environmental destruction, to mass-media coverage of events, trends, and ideas, to telecommunications capabilities. It is an era of technological revolution and information explosion. Therefore public issues are increasingly complicated, and multiply connected with other issues at the levels of cause, process, and effect. If citizens are to be able to participate in public deliberations and actions on these issues, they must have a more sophisticated understanding of them.

For example, students could participate in thematic studies, investigating the treatment of problems or issues from the perspectives of various academic disciplines. They could also look at an issue comparatively, as it manifests itself and is addressed in different countries or cultures. Students could also gain insight into global interdependence by studying the actions and policies of individual nations and major corporations, and some of their consequences for people in those and other societies.

As another aspect of their need to increase their knowledge of the complexities of major public issues, students must also gain enough knowledge of science, and the nature of the construction of scientific knowledge, to develop the self-confidence to make their own evaluations of public issues related to science and technology. An important part of such education is the study of the relationships between science/technology and society—how each shapes and affects the other.

---

23. Paulo Freire, *Pedagogy of the Oppressed*, 67.

Understanding the Social Construction of Knowledge and Developing Students' Self-Confidence in their Own Role in Knowledge Construction. The idea that science is influenced and shaped by society, and that science in turn shapes society, is based on the larger notion of the social construction of knowledge. A key step in the education of young people for public democratic citizenship takes place when they grasp the insight that all knowledge—that which they carry around in their heads, as well as that which they confront in their schoolwork and in the larger world—is socially constructed.[24]

Students need to be aware that whatever text they study—be it a news report, a piece of literature or art, a historical article, an advertisement, or a political or scientific argument—is a socially constructed text, representing particular points of view or ideological positions that can be identified and discussed. Moreover, the meaning of a given text is "not restricted to a single, harmonious and authoritative reading."[25] It could be open to any number of interpretations or "readings." Since texts are open to a variety of interpretations or readings based in part on the positions or experience of readers, students' present knowledge becomes an important resource upon which they can draw when confronting new knowledge.

For this reason, students' own knowledge must be validated in school, and actively brought to bear in the learning process. Students should be encouraged to make connections between their previous knowledge, including that which they have acquired in their experiences with family, peer groups, mass media, and other aspects of their daily lives, and the new knowledge that they encounter in their schoolwork. Such an approach is cognitively effective, in that in order to make sense of any new information, students must organize it in terms of their own existing knowledge bases.[26] Teachers should take advantage of this fact and actively encourage students to make such connections.

Validating students' own knowledge and helping them make new knowledge their own also gives students a sense of their own voice. It gives students a sense of intellectual self-confidence. They recognize

---

24. Vito Perrone, *A Letter to Teachers* (San Francisco: Josey-Bass Publishers, 1991), 29.

25. Catherine Belsey, *Critical Practice* (New York: Methuen, 1980), 104; quoted in Giroux, *Schooling and the Struggle for a Public Life*, 139.

26. Jean Piaget, *The Development of Thought: Equilibration of Cognitive Structures* (New York: Viking Press, 1977).

their own agency as intellectual actors, and thus their potential as independent social and political actors.

However, the knowledge students bring with them to school should not simply be accepted at face value and celebrated. It must also be "interrogated critically with respect to the ideologies it contains, the means of representation it utilizes, and the underlying social practices it confirms."[27] The idea is to help students better understand how their socially constituted knowledge and beliefs support and are supported by existing social relations and structures of power in society. By becoming more aware of the connections between their knowledge and the structures of power in society, young people open up the possibility of taking action to transform both the state of their own knowledge and existing social relations.

Learning to Direct One's Own Learning.   One of the most vital capacities that schools can nurture in young people is the ability to act as self-educating individuals. The ability to direct their own learning enables young citizens to keep themselves informed about important issues that arise in their personal lives and in society.[28] The development of this ability requires thoughtful, guided practice. Schools should therefore offer students a multitude of opportunities to take control of their own learning. Schools should take seriously "students' questions and deep interests, using them as starting points for the content being examined."[29] They should make resources available to students, and provide guidance in using them and in finding other resources to enable them to investigate their interests.

Students who take charge of their own learning take the first step toward taking control of their lives. They develop an ability to confront new circumstances, information, issues, and ideas with power—the power to study, analyze, and understand. Understanding a situation is the condition for rational, democratic action. Maximizing student choice and control over their own activities for intellectual exploration and growth is one of the primary components of a democratic vision of schooling.[30]

---

27. Henry Giroux, *Schooling and Struggle for Public Life*, 143.

28. Dewey, *Democracy and Education*, 51–53, 99; Mills, *Power, Politics and People*, 367–68.

29. Vito Perrone, 27. See also John Dewey, *Democracy and Education*, 155.

30. Dewey, *Democracy and Education*, 304–5.

Modeling Participation in Democratic Schools

Joseph Grannis argues that "every school represents to its students a model of society and its possibilities."[31] Therefore to the extent that democratic practices are built into everyday school life, students are presented with living models of the possibilities and the difficulties of democratic political activity. By example and through personal experience students have the opportunity to develop some of the basic capacities for public democratic citizenship. If educators truly wish to help students develop their democratic capacities, schools should be organized so that students, teachers, and parents have opportunities to participate democratically in the life of the school.

Students can have a voice in many important aspects of the organization of school life. Meaningful participation in the processes of decision-making in public institutions provides the best preparation for further public democratic activity. As Benjamin Barber puts it, "politics becomes its own university, citizenship its own training ground, and participation its own tutor."[32] Since the public school is for most people the first public institution they will know, and the one they come to know most intimately, through their own educational careers and those of their children, it is one of the best places for young people to begin to exercise their democratic rights and responsibilities.

I will not attempt to prescribe any specific plans for incorporating students into school decision-making processes. This can be done to varying degrees and in many different ways. Each school that seeks actively to prepare students for democratic citizenship will want to deal with the issue of student participation in school governance in its own way. But the issue is one that should not be neglected.

Another way of building democratic practices into school life involves teachers taking greater control of the way their work lives are defined, structured, and organized. This means, in the first place,

---

31. Joseph C. Grannis, "The School as a Model of Society," in *The Learning of Political Behavior*, ed. Norman Adler and Charles Harrington (Glenview, IL: Scott, Foresman and Co., 1970), 137.

32. Barber, *Strong Democracy*, 152. It is surprising and disappointing that in what is otherwise a thoughtful and compelling book, Barber practically ignores the issue of the role of formal education in his vision of a "strong democracy."

that teachers, and not just administrators or textbook publishers, should play central roles in collaboratively defining and coordinating the various parts of the curriculum they will teach; choosing the materials they will use and make available to students; and deciding how to organize and guide their students' intellectual and social development. This also means that teachers should have a voice in deciding how school resources are allocated to best provide for students' needs. Moreover, teachers should have meaningful input into the way classes are scheduled, their assignments to classrooms, and the making of school policies and rules. A school that is run democratically by teachers provides a model of the complications and the rewards of participation in democratic processes.

Finally, parents, whenever possible, should also be involved in their children's schooling. Parents have a strong personal stake in their children's future. In most cases, parents already are the primary educators of their children. They are their children's first and most constant teachers, as well as their strongest role models for adulthood and, indeed, for citizenship. They are in a strong position to support their children's formal education through the attitudes they project about schooling in general, their children's school and teachers, and schoolwork; and through the concrete ways they intervene in their children's educational experience, such as by monitoring their academic and personal progress and working to help teachers understand and address children's individual needs.

In addition to all the above ways that parents can participate in their children's education, they should also have a voice in the school governance process. This touches on some volatile issues, even among many progressive educators. At the first mention of parent roles in school governance, questions of educational professionalism, academic freedom, and teacher and administrator job security arise. However, if schools are to be public institutions that help prepare young people for public democratic life, then parents must have some voice in how their children's schools are run.

Clearly not all parents are able to participate in school governance because of the pressures of their everyday lives. And if parents feel that their school is serving their children well, they will often be happy to leave school governance to the professionals. Furthermore, when students get to the high school level, they often don't want their parents to become deeply involved in their schools. This is sometimes because adolescents want to be treated as the adults they almost are, and be allowed to take responsibility for their school lives; and it is sometimes because of established norms in many high schools in which a parent's presence in the school is automatically assumed to be in connection with a serious academic or disciplinary problem that the student is having.

However, there are several reasons why schools should have institutionalized channels through which parents can get involved in school governance. First, when it becomes clear that a school is not working for many young people, and that it is not doing anything visibly to improve the situation, parents must be able to intervene. Second, even in a generally functional school, problems can arise which are best resolved with input from parents. Third, particularly in urban schools where teachers and administrators are predominantly European-American and students are mostly Latino, African-American, or Asian, parents should be involved in the school in order to insure that cultural diversity is respected and that the children are well served. Finally, parent involvement in school governance can provide students with a tangible and compelling vision of the possibility of public democratic participation by ordinary people from their own families and communities.

It is clear that most schools do not take it as their mission to adopt many of the organizational features, or the educational practices that have been identified in this chapter as necessary for promoting students' development as active and effective citizens of a democracy. However, for those educators who aspire to create schools that promote public democratic citizenship, it is important to have a way of assessing the practices of their own or other schools in terms of the degree to which they approach this goal.

This chapter has sketched the outlines of an ideal-typical secondary school for public democracy. This ideal image, rough as it is, can be used as a tool for examining and analyzing the organization and practices of existing schools. By comparing the organization and practices of real schools to the ideal-typical school outlined here, it will be possible to see the degree to which various aspects of the real schools promote (or fail to promote) the values, attributes, and capacities that have been identified as necessary for public democratic citizenship.

In part II of this book, this analytical tool will be applied in some sample analyses of a few organizational features and educational practices of two existing urban alternative public high schools.

PART II

Democratic Education?
Tales from Two Schools

As part I of this book argues, if we in the United States hope to begin to reverse the processes of social decay and political alienation that increasingly define American social life, it will be necessary to redefine and revitalize our conception of democratic citizenship. We will need to build an alternative vision and practice of public democratic citizenship that will challenge and supplant the privatized conception of democracy that now dominates the collective American political imagination.

Educators can play a role in creating this new public vision and practice of democracy by helping young people develop the values, attributes, and capacities necessary for public democratic citizenship. Many publicly minded educators have already undertaken this task in democratically restructured schools throughout the country. To strengthen and nurture this movement for public democratic education, educators must be able to assess the development of these schools as institutions which prepare young people for public democratic citizenship. By studying the organization and practices of existing democratic schools, educators inside and outside of these schools can better understand what it takes to create and sustain education for public democratic citizenship.

The second half of this book offers a description and analysis of a few key aspects of two urban alternative public high schools, which were the focus of field research during the spring 1990 and spring 1991 academic terms. The reason for studying high schools, rather than middle or elementary schools, is that high school marks a kind of stepping off point for students to adulthood and citizenship. Since schooling is mandatory to the age of 16 in most states, high school is the last publicly controlled institution where socialization for citizenship can be expected to occur for many young people. The two high schools selected for this study represent promising educational models for preparing young people for effective public democratic citizenship.

The research on these two high schools employed a variety of methods: ethnographic observations, examination of school publications, curriculum documents, and pamphlets, formal and informal interviews of staff members and students, and in one of the schools, focus group interviews with students. Although some standard ethnographic methods were used, this study differs from a traditional ethnography in a crucial sense. This is not a closed-system study of the socially constructed cultures of these two individual schools. This study utilizes a structured framework for analyzing the schools, in a way which links it to the larger historical struggle between privatizing and public ideologies and practices of democracy. The theoretical framework and the ideal-type elaborated in part I of this book make it possible to systematically analyze selected aspects of the organization, curriculum, and teaching practices of the two schools, to find out to what degree they engage their students in education for public democratic citizenship.

It should be emphasized, however, that the framework for analysis was not simply imposed a priori on the study. Naturally, I went into these schools as a researcher with some general, preconceived ideas about what constitutes democratic citizenship and democratic education. But a conscious effort was made to record students' and teachers' accounts of their school experiences, not in terms of my ideas on democratic education, but rather as they saw and interpreted them in their own terms. Only after most of the field work was completed did I begin to construct the theoretical framework for analyzing the school data. This was a dialectical process. It drew both on the focused readings of democratic and educational theory discussed in part I, and on insights provided by the school data, which forced important additions and modifications in the emerging theoretical framework, as new or more precise analytical categories suggested themselves.

It also must be noted that this study does not attempt to offer a complete ethnographic description of either school. Rather, it presents a description and analysis of important aspects of the organization, curriculum, and teaching practices in the two schools. The study then looks in some detail at two exemplary classes, one in each school. The classes are analyzed in terms of the ways in which they promote student engagement and development of public democratic values and capacities. The analysis of these two classes leads to discussion of student responses to key aspects of the overall organization and practices of the two schools.

The purpose is not to thoroughly critique the two schools as models of public democratic education. It is to analyze selected formal and informal features of the schools in some depth, to see what can be learned about the complexities of creating democratic education. An additional, equally important purpose is to demonstrate the usefulness of the theoretically defined framework employed here as a tool for analyzing various aspects of schools that aspire to public democratic education. College-based teacher educators, public school educators, and parents who wish to promote democratic education in their own schools and communities, can utilize this framework of analysis to examine and assess the successes and shortcomings of their efforts.

Three main questions are addressed in the analysis of the two schools in this study. First, to what extent do the organization and educational practices of these two schools coincide with those identified in part I as contributing to student engagement, and to students' development of public democratic values, attributes, and capacities? Second, to what degree are students engaged in the relevant school practices? Third, are there signs that students are taking on some of the values, attributes, and capacities necessary for public democratic citizenship?

CHAPTER 6

Structure and Organization of Two Democratic High Schools

The two alternative high schools in this study are located in a city in the eastern United States. As a condition for doing the research on these two schools, the names of the schools and the city in which they are located, will not be revealed. Instead, the schools will be referred to as Uptown High School (UHS) and Metropolitan High School (MHS), and the city will be called Metro City.

Alternative high schools have had a place in the Metro City public school system since the early 1970s. There are a number of alternative public high schools, offering a wide variety of programs. They cannot easily be characterized as a group, except to say, as the Metro City Board of Education puts it in one of its school directories, they offer "high school diploma programs for students who may benefit from an option different from that offered in the traditional high school." In addition, they tend to be significantly smaller than traditional high schools, and are often housed in school-within-a-school settings, allowing for a more "personalized atmosphere" than that available in larger schools.

I spent one to two days a week at Uptown High School, from January through June 1990, observing classes and staff meetings, and conducting formal and informal interviews with students and teachers. A series of follow-up observations and interviews were

111

conducted in the spring of 1991. At Metropolitan High School, I spent a day and a half a week from February through May 1991. I observed classes and conducted formal and informal interviews with students and teachers. In addition, I conducted three formal focus groups with students on their perceptions of the educational experience at Metropolitan H.S. During the months following my field research at the school, I conducted interviews and had extended telephone conversations with the school's co-directors, to flesh out my understanding of the overall operation of the school.

Both Uptown H.S. and Metropolitan H.S. are members of a national network of restructured secondary schools. They share a commitment to a number of the network's basic educational and philosophical principles, which will be described later. The fact that both Uptown and Metropolitan High Schools serve an inner-city population of young people of color make them especially important case-study schools. If they are indeed able to provide an effective public democratic education to these students, they will be opening a new door—the door to empowered citizenship—to these members of traditionally disenfranchised groups.

Uptown High School Background and Goals

Uptown High School is an alternative public high school in a low-income and working-class Latino and African-American neighborhood. Uptown High School's students are drawn primarily from the surrounding community, with only 25 percent coming from outside the neighborhood surrounding the school. Almost half come to Uptown High School from one of several local alternative public elementary schools. The Uptown H.S. student body is 43 percent African-American, 37 percent Latino, and 20 percent European-American or Asian.

Uptown is a small high school, with about 450 students in all. It is organized into three divisions or sections: the Lower Section comprises the seventh and eighth grades; the Middle Section is the ninth and tenth grades; and the Upper Section is comprised of the eleventh and twelfth grades. When I began the study in January of 1990, the school encompassed grades 7–11. The first seniors graduated in June of 1991, as I completed my field research.

During the 1989–90 school year Uptown High School had a staff of about forty teachers. The teaching staff had about twenty each men and women, and was approximately 69 percent European-American, 21 percent African-American, and 10 percent Latino. Some teachers had many years experience in Metro City public schools. A number of others had been recruited from teaching in respected, progressive private schools. Upon taking teaching positions at Uptown H.S., all the teachers made a commitment to dedicate themselves to the formidable task of helping create and run the school, from curriculum design to teaching to administrative decision-making.

The principal and founder of Uptown H.S., Maria Landon,[1] is widely recognized as an educational leader and innovator. Although Maria Landon is the school's principal and overall director, accountable to local and state educational authorities, Uptown High School is a faculty-run school. Most major school policy decisions are made by an assembly of the staff, in their weekly staff meetings.

Uptown H.S. seeks to educate its students for both intellectual development and for public democratic participation. It seeks to develop in each student rigorous "habits of mind" with which to understand the world.[2] These habits of mind should enable students to analyze any information or ideas they encounter, by

1. Identifying the viewpoint or perspective that is being expressed;
2. Evaluating available evidence;
3. Seeing connections with other relevant information, ideas, events, or issues;
4. Imagining other alternatives; and
5. Understanding the broad significance of the subject.[3]

Students who develop these habits of mind will be "thoughtful, critical, and educated," that is, the kind of citizens upon which democracy depends. To the extent that it is successful, Uptown H.S. is "educating citizens for a powerful democracy."[4]

---

1. This is a pseudonym, as are the names of all the people referred to in this study.
2. Interview with Ruth Smith, Humanities Team Leader for UHS Lower and Middle Sections, 19 March 1990.
3. Uptown High School pamphlet.
4. Interview with Ruth Smith, 19 March 1990.

Uptown H.S. subscribes to the guiding principles of the Coalition of Essential Schools, a national network of restructured secondary schools, of which it is a member.[5] These principles help shape the forms of teaching and learning, as well as the organizational structure of the school. These principles include the following:

1. Personalization. Although the course of study is unified and universal, teaching and learning is [sic] personalized. No teacher is responsible for teaching more than 80 students, or for advising more than 15.
2. Less is more. It is more important to know some things well than to know many things superficially.
3. Goal Setting. High standards are set for all students. Students must clearly exhibit mastery of their schoolwork.
4. Student-as-Worker. . . . Teachers "coach" students, encouraging students to find answers and to, in effect, teach themselves. Thus students discover answers and solutions, and learn by doing rather than by simply repeating what text books (or teachers) say.[6]

Metropolitan High School Background and Goals

The second alternative high school is Metropolitan High School (MHS). With its approximately one hundred students, Metropolitan

---

5. As of 1 March 1994, the Coalition of Essential Schools (CES) network included 156 member schools along with 97 "Planning Schools" (which intended to apply for membership shortly) and 461 "Exploring Schools" (which were actively studying the coalition's principles for school change) ("Information on Member Schools," Coalition of Essential Schools fact sheet, 1 March 94).

CES schools are committed to creating thoroughly new designs for American secondary-school education, to improve student learning and achievement. CES was founded as a high school–university partnership in 1984 at Brown University by Theodore Sizer, who continues as its chairman. The ideas behind CES are explored in two of Sizer's books, *Horace's Compromise* (Boston: Houghton Mifflin Co., 1985) and *Horace's School* (Boston: Houghton Mifflin Co., 1992).

For a thoughtful, if pessimistic, discussion of the CES reform movement, see Richard A. Gibboney, *The Stone Trumpet* (Albany, NY: SUNY Press, 1994), 62–72. Based on my research in the two CES schools in this book, I am more optimistic than Gibboney about the potential for success of the CES reform program, among its slowly expanding group of member schools.

6. Uptown High School pamphlet.

High School is much smaller even than Uptown High School. It is housed within one three-floor wing of a traditional comprehensive high school. MHS draws its students from all over the city. The students are a diverse group in terms of racial and ethnic background. Seventy-five to eighty percent of the students split into approximately equal numbers of African-Americans and Latinos. About 20 percent of the students are of European descent, and a very small percentage are of Asian descent. According to co-director Michael Bell, the students are mostly from low-income families. They come to Metropolitan High School having dropped out or nearly dropped out of other city high schools. Bell characterizes MHS students as bright young people who have been turned off by traditional high schools.

Like Uptown High School (UHS), Metropolitan High School is a staff-run school. Its co-directors, Michael Bell and Karen Meese are responsible for the day-to-day administration of the school, all dealings with city and state education authorities, and public relations appearances and activities for the school. In addition to their administrative work, they also teach at least one class each semester.

The staff of Metropolitan High School consists of seven full-time teachers/staff developers plus administrative and support staff. Five of MHS's full-time teaching faculty are of European-American descent, one is African-American and one is Latino. Four of the teachers are men and three are women.

Along with their work at Metropolitan H.S., these teachers are all involved in the staff development work of an inquiry learning project. This project involves a team of educators working with groups of teachers in a number of schools throughout Metro City, to develop innovative teaching practices. The project seeks to study teaching and learning by looking at *how* young people learn, not just *what* they have learned. Teachers and the project team work together to build teaching practices around how students actually learn.

Metropolitan H.S.'s inquiry learning orientation puts students as researchers at the center of the learning process. Students are encouraged to "explore ideas, conduct research, evaluate information, discuss ideas respectfully, develop new sources of fact and opinion, [and] present and defend their findings."[7] These goals are in the

---

7. Metropolitan H.S. pamphlet.

same spirit as the "habits of mind" that Uptown H.S. attempts to nurture in its students. MHS, like UHS, is a member of the coalition of Essential Schools, and subscribes to coalition principles such as personalization, less is more, goal setting, and student-as-worker.

A major goal for MHS is to help students recognize that there are ambiguities in all human events, and that they will have to "think through issues," argue about them, and take positions based on evidence they gather.[8] The school explicitly rejects a vision of education that sees young people as "vessels to pour knowledge into." For Michael Bell,

> there is information kids need, and we don't deny that and don't ignore it, but the information is a means to an end. How you acquire it, and what you do with it, is what's important.[9]

This approach to education is connected to Bell's vision of the kind of citizenship education that Metropolitan H.S. provides. Bell explains his vision as follows:

> What we're trying to do is develop thoughtful individuals who are prepared to make judgments, support judgments with evidence and act on judgments. Now, depending on what your definition of good citizenship is, I mean, if you want a citizenry that will follow orders, be good army men, and vote in an election because Tweedle Dee and Tweedle Dum are running, we're not creating a good citizen. [But] if you want someone who is critical and questioning, ... if we're really successful, that's what we're creating.[10]

Bell feels that the kind of citizen Metropolitan H.S. is trying to develop is "someone who's analytical, critical, and thoughtful"; but one who uses reasoned criticism, "not [someone who's] just yelling at the top of a building."[11] MHS "help[s] students become good citizens who value civil debate, and can and will engage in making informed choices for our nation."[12]

---

8. Interview with MHS co-director Michael Bell, 2 July 1991.
9. Ibid.
10. Ibid.
11. Ibid.
12. Metropolitan H.S. pamphlet.

Student Engagement and Preparation for
Public Democratic Citizenship

Several features of the organization of UHS and MHS need to be examined more closely to determine the extent to which they are likely to engage students, and help them develop public democratic values, attributes, and capacities. Part I of this book enumerated several school characteristics likely to engage students in its educational programs (see table 5.1, p. 87). It also laid out a series of ideal school practices for nurturing public democratic qualities in young people (see table 5.2, p. 89). These school characteristics and practices serve as a standard against which to compare and analyze some of the characteristics and practices of the two schools in this study.

For analytical clarity in part I, school characteristics that promote student engagement were discussed separately from school practices that nurture public democratic values, attributes, and capacities. However, this is something of a false distinction. Several of the school characteristics that enhance student engagement lead naturally to democratic educational practices, just as many school practices that promote democratic thinking and action are by their nature highly engaging to students.

For the purpose of ordering this discussion, I will start with the characteristics of Uptown H.S. and Metropolitan H.S. that are likely to encourage student engagement. However, the discussion will often flow directly into an analysis of school practices that nurture public democratic values, attributes and capacities. Because of this natural blending of analytical categories I will not deal systematically and separately with all the ideal school practices. Rather, I will talk about democratic school practices as they arise in the discussion of the characteristics of each school that encourage student engagement.

I will now turn my attention to the first two school characteristics that are likely to engage students in their school programs.

Student Engagement: Membership and Safety
in the School Community

A theme that came up repeatedly in observations and conversations with students and teachers in both UHS and MHS was the importance of relationships. Relationships between students and teachers, as well as among students and among teachers, give rise to feelings of community, of family, and of home. The tone that is set by these feelings brings together the first two characteristics that are likely to engage students in the life and work of a school: (1) an atmosphere in which students feel a sense of belonging or membership; and (2) an environment that feels safe for students, both physically and emotionally. Such an atmosphere becomes a source of strength that underlies the success of these schools.

School Size

The atmosphere of belonging or membership is cultivated through several of the structural/organizational features of both schools. One of the most important of these is size—both schools are quite small compared to traditional comprehensive Metro City high schools.

One way in which UHS institutionalizes "smallness" and nurtures an atmosphere of student belonging and membership in the school community is through its "house" system. UHS's Lower and Middle Sections (comprising grades 7–8 and 9–10 respectively) are each divided into two mixed-grade "houses" of seventy-five to eighty students. Each house has a faculty team of five teachers, which includes experts in English, history, math, science, and art.[13] This arrangement limits the number of *different* students a given teacher sees on a regular basis to the number in the house (a maximum of 80). It allows a group of teachers to get to know a group of students very well over the course of the two years students are in a particular house. Every student can be known by her/his teachers, and s/he can get to know them. The organization of Uptown H.S. into distinct sections and houses reinforces the sense that students belong to a specific community within the larger community of the school.

MHS promotes students' sense of belonging and membership by maintaining its overall small size. There is no need to break down into "houses" because the total population of the school is essentially a house of one hundred students and seven teachers.

---

13. Uptown H.S. Handbook.

The smallness of the schools and their subdivisions creates the possibility for regular personal contact among students and teachers. This is a requisite for developing caring relationships, which are the heart of true school community. As Michelle Fine states,

> If voices are to flourish inside public high schools, then those institutions need to be small, personal and organized around relationships between students and adults, as well as among adults. . . . Although small size is never sufficient, large anonymous structures will never do if we are interested in creating a sense of community and connection.[14]

Students in both schools commented on another small but significant contributor to their sense of membership in a close school community. In both UHS and MHS, students call teachers by their first names. As Jose, a Metropolitan H.S. student expressed it, "One thing is, it's informal here. Like we call teachers by their first names. They don't mind. And in class it's not like a teacher-student relationship. It's like person to person."[15]

Advisory Systems

A system of student advisories in each school serves some of the same relationship and community-building purposes. At Uptown H.S., every student is assigned to an advisory group of no more than fifteen students. The teacher or staff member who leads this group acts as the students' academic advisor, unofficial counselor, and advocate. If a student is having a problem in school, or even out of school, the advisor is a person to whom the student can turn. Likewise, if another teacher sees that a student is having trouble—academically or otherwise—that teacher goes to the student's advisor, who will work with the student, and when appropriate, the student's parents, to help resolve the problem.

The advisory class meets on a daily basis, offering students the opportunity to discuss current school concerns; to explore issues of

---

14. Michelle Fine, 220.
15. Field notes, 9 April 1991.

importance to students in such areas as family, health, sex education, ethics, current events, and public life; or simply to read, write
in student journals, study, or get some extra help on projects or
assignments. It is also a time when students can meet individually
with the advisor to discuss personal or academic concerns, problems, or plans. Advisory classes also take trips, including a visit
each year to a college campus, to expose students to a number of
possible college options.

Advisory classes at Metropolitan H.S. also contribute to a family/
community atmosphere in the school. These classes, which generally
meet once a week for an hour, serve a purpose similar to that of
advisory classes at Uptown H.S. Within the safe environment of the
advisory group, students have the opportunity to explore a range of
issues of importance to them, such as health, sex education, college
and career possibilities, or other school, personal or social concerns.
Once a month, advisory groups also take trips to colleges and other
places of interest both in and out of Metro City.

The regular meetings and personal development focus of advisory
classes, as well as the institutionalization of an adult mentoring role
that is the result of the advisor-student relationship, reinforce the
degree to which teachers know the students personally and come to
truly care about them. An illustration of this occurred during a
break in an Uptown H.S. Upper Section class I observed. As the
students left the classroom for a short break, Nancy Richards, a
coordinator of community service and senior internships, came in to
speak with Joan Mitchell, the teacher whose class I was observing.

> *Nancy:* I just wanted you to know T and R Company called.
> They said Ana said she wasn't feeling well. I told them to keep
> her there. I was very firm. [T and R is this student's internship
> placement.]
>
> *Joan:* Did she say what was wrong?
>
> *Nancy:* No.
>
> *Joan:* So you think she was just going to meet that guy? I'll call
> her tonight. Thanks for being firm with her.
>
> [Joan tells me about the girl—one of her advisory students—
> and the girl's relationship with her parents. The student has

been kept very sheltered, but she's been getting around her restrictions.]

Joan: Ana is 17 and she's never been out anywhere without the parents or her sister. Or so the parents think. So of course she finds ways, creative ways, to get around it. . . . (Field notes, 18 April 1991)

It was clear that this brief interaction was part of an ongoing process of dealing with a student whose personal life was affecting her schoolwork, in this case her work in her senior internship. The advisor was apparently in touch with the student, the family, and the student's other teachers, and was working to intervene in what she saw as the student's best interest. This advisor was close enough to the student and the family to know the background of the situation, set up a plan with the internship coordinator to "be firm" with the student, and follow up with a phone call to the student that evening to discuss the situation further. This incident offers a small example of the degree to which advisory systems in these two schools can help caring teacher-student-family relationships to develop.

Class Size

Small class size also helps students and teachers come to know each other well and develop a sense of community. Class size at UHS is kept to a maximum of eighteen students. Class size at MHS is also kept small, in accordance with the Metro City mandated average of sixteen students for alternative high school classes. Some MHS classes are larger than the average, so that other classes, such as those taught by newer staff members and those which particularly benefit from smaller student/teacher ratios (such as science labs), can be kept smaller.[16]

Class sizes can be maintained at these levels not because of more generous per-pupil funding for alternative high schools. In fact, Metro City alternative high schools are funded at a lower per-pupil rate than traditional comprehensive high schools. In alternative schools,

---

16. Karen Meese, in a phone conversation, 15 November 1992.

administrative costs are kept lower than in regular high schools. For example, Metropolitan H.S. has no specially funded department chair positions and no one funded at a principal's salary. The principal's position is funded at an assistant principal's rate. Because the advisory systems in both MHS and UHS replace the traditional guidance counselor system, and because Uptown H.S. employs fewer other non-teaching administrative staff than most schools, proportionally more staff members can be devoted strictly to teaching than in traditional schools. With more teachers teaching fewer classes, class sizes can be kept well below the average class size in a traditional Metro City public high school, which ranges from twenty-eight in vocational high schools to thirty-four in regular comprehensive high schools.

According to Karen Meese, these are typical staff funding arrangements for Metro City alternative high schools. So in effect, UHS and MHS are able to provide small classes even while operating at comparable or even lower per-pupil funding levels than traditional Metro City high schools.[17]

Physical Space

Another factor that can contribute to creating a humane, personable atmosphere and a sense of community is the organization of the school's physical space. This can be seen, for example, in the use of school space at Metropolitan H.S. Although its classrooms are spread out on three different floors in its host school building, MHS has a center of gravity in a suite of two large adjoining rooms on the first floor. One room is the office, where the co-directors and staff members have their desks, piled high with books, photocopied articles, folders, and other materials of the teaching trade. There are posters and cartoons on the walls, several telephones, a couple of MacIntosh computers, a copy machine, storage closets for books and other materials and staff mail folders. Students all have lockers against the office wall nearest to the doorway to the adjoining room. Students are constantly coming into the office to get to their lockers.

---

17. Ibid.

The second room serves as a reading/relaxation lounge for students and teachers. It has a large conference-style table and chairs, and a couple of small couches against the walls. There's a sink, a refrigerator, and a magazine rack loaded with newspapers and popular magazines. Students hang out in the lounge before school starts and between classes, and many eat their lunches there or come to hang out there and socialize for at least part of the lunch period.

Michael Bell's desk is located right next to the doorway between the two rooms. His chair is practically in the doorway. As students come in, he marks their attendance for the day. If he doesn't see them in the morning, and sees them later, he asks them where they've been and checks to see if everything's all right. He makes sure they're not sick or having a problem, and reminds them how important it is to be in school. He really knows all the students well, it seems. The other teachers also seem to know the students well and take a personal interest in them. The physical set-up, combined with the obviously high level of personal interest and concern staff members have for the students, makes for an environment in which students feel at home. As Michael Bell sees it,

> This is a small office, and we're all in one room for a real purpose. We are instantly accessible to each other all the time. And the kids will wander in and find us very easily. And they have to because their lockers are here. There's a lot of informal interaction.

One of the important benefits of this structurally guaranteed, ongoing informal interaction between students and teachers in the office/locker suite is that students see some of the work that goes into making their school function. They see what it takes to run their school in terms of pulling together materials for creative, inquiry-based teaching; making phone calls and writing letters to arrange for special trips and visiting speakers; meetings among staff members on curriculum and teaching issues; and so on. Perhaps most importantly, students witness first hand one of the central, complex dynamics of their school's operation: the effort the staff makes to run the school as a fully collaborative endeavor.[18] All of this adds to a sense of intimacy and connection among teachers and students in the shared construction of the students' education.

---

18. Ibid.

Caring Teachers

In part, no doubt, because of the relationships that develop among teachers and students in UHS and MHS, students from both schools feel that their teachers display a sincerity and personal interest for their students in even the most academic contexts. This also contributes to creating a caring environment in the school. An illustration of this was offered to me by Theresa, an Uptown H.S. student who commented on the individual effort teachers make to help students.

> The teachers really care about students here. Once I was having a lot of trouble with calculus. But I have dance after school. So Veronica [her math teacher] says, "It's no problem, you can meet me at 7:15 for extra help." But 7:15! I ended up meeting her at 7:30. . . . But the teachers are like that.[19]

Physical and Emotional Safety

The smallness of the school, the caring environment, the structured and the informal relationships that develop between teachers and students and among students themselves—all these contribute to creating school environments that are physically safe. When people know each other in a school there is automatically some sense of accountability. And when there is a feeling of care, the likelihood diminishes of people acting irresponsibly or violently toward other members of the school community. So it can be argued that Uptown H.S. and Metropolitan H.S. are inherently safer environments than many large urban high schools.

Still, conflicts can occur and people can act irresponsibly toward others or toward other people's property. One way that Uptown H.S. deals with this reality is that many of its staff and students have received training in conflict resolution, and there is an active peer mediation program in place. This program provides a safe, structured, mediated process of communication between students who have a conflict. Through the mediation process, students can calmly discuss their conflict, and devise mutually agreed upon solu-

---

19. Field notes, 18 April 1991.

tions that will defuse the conflict and prevent it from surfacing again.[20]

Beyond the question of physical safety, it is also important for a school to provide an atmosphere of emotional safety and support for students, so that they will feel free to express themselves, take risks, try new ideas, and make mistakes from which they will learn. There was evidence of this in several class discussions I observed.

One example comes from the Metropolitan H.S. novels class. In this class students are all reading different novels of their choice. They spend some time each class sharing and discussing their stories, and some of the issues and themes that arise from their reading. The rest of the class time is used for reading, journal writing about their reading, and writing up novel cards that tell a little bit about books students have read, and make recommendations to other students about whether they're worth reading. One day, a student was telling the class about the novel she was reading, *The Good Mother,* by Sue Miller. She related a part in the book when the four-year-old daughter of the main character was in the bathroom as her mother's boyfriend was getting out of the shower. The little girl wanted to touch the mother's boyfriend's penis. The telling of this incident from the book sparked a long class discussion on the issue of talking to children about sex. Here are excerpts from my field notes from that class.

> Chris [the teacher] initially guides the discussion, getting students to talk about their feelings about when children should be taught about sex, how to deal with children's curiosity when they touch others' private parts, etc. Maria describes her history of how she learned about sex—from other students, from her older sister and brother—but *not* from her parents. From this, further discussion follows about when it's appropriate to teach children about sex, what to do when little kids start "playing doctor," and so on. . . .
>
> It was a very stimulating, serious discussion. Students talked about a very sensitive subject with intelligence and maturity. Most of the students (at least six of the ten students present)

---

20. Field notes, 13 February 1990, UHS teacher discussing conflict resolution program with group of visitors.

took an active part in the discussion, often speaking out simultaneously to try to make their thoughts heard.

The discussion that went back and forth between Freddy and David (with others listening closely and often joining in) was especially good. At one point, David said to Freddy, "Explain to me what you would say to the kid" [i.e., explain to the child who's getting into "playing doctor" why not to do it and what sex is about]. "I'll be the four-year-old and you be the father. What would you say?"

At first Freddy was a bit mixed up in explaining what he'd do and say. But through the discussion, he gradually began sorting out his thoughts. . . . He wouldn't be able to explain everything about sex to a four-year-old. But he also couldn't just hit the child and tell her to stop [which is what he had said he would do at first]. He'd have to explain somewhat to her why she shouldn't do that, and maybe begin to explain something about the body.[21]

In this class, students used the springboard of an incident in a novel, and related it to their own experiences and to what they might do in the future, as parents, with their own children. It was clear that the discussion participants were listening to each other, since there was a distinct evolution of Freddy's thinking as he discussed the issue with his classmates. In addition, although the teacher initially led the discussion, students soon took control, speaking and responding directly to each other, without mediation from the teacher. This kind of discussion among adolescents, dealing seriously and sensitively with a subject as personal as how to talk to young children about their bodies and about sex, could only take place in a classroom environment in which students feel truly comfortable and safe.

Jose, a Metropolitan H.S. student, offers another example that summarizes how the feeling of care, of closeness, and of belonging comes across in the relationships between teachers and students at his school. He spoke to me briefly as he waited in the office for a friend who was going out to lunch with him.

---

21. Field notes, 19 March 1991.

Jose: Have you talked to Michael [Bell] about the school?

DS: No, well only a little bit.

Jose: You gotta talk to Michael. He gives so much to the students. Out of his own pocket. Just in [public transit] tokens alone. He must go through about two packs of tokens a day. And he's not getting that money back. Or maybe he is, but he doesn't know that for sure.

And everybody's like that around here. If I asked Chris [a teacher who is passing by right at that moment] to lend me a few bucks, he'd give it to me if he had it. Right, Chris?

[Chris smiles and says yes.]

See that? And so would any of the teachers. We're close here. WE ARE FAMILY. Put that in your thesis.[22]

This feeling of school as family and community is one of the outstanding qualities one can't help but notice in Uptown and Metropolitan High Schools. It is important to emphasize that this feeling doesn't develop by accident, and it doesn't come about simply because there is an extraordinarily dedicated and gifted group of teachers in each of these schools. The schools are structured and organized to nurture the kinds of relationships that create feelings of belonging, connection, and care. No doubt the structuring of school life around such relationships, combined with the fact that teachers in these schools are given room to function as the professionals that they are, helps to motivate the kind of dedication and creativity that mark these faculties as special. It also creates a marvelous and engaging environment for the education and growth of high school students.

Promoting an Ethic of Care

The benefits of organizing these schools around relationships that promote a sense of belonging and care go beyond creating an engaging atmosphere for learning. The organization of these schools

22. Field notes, 9 April 1991.

also models, and therefore promotes, through students' lived experience in the schools, an ethic of care and responsibility. The ethic of care and responsibility that permeates these schools brings home to students the importance of developing themselves as individuals, but always within a context of their connections with others through relationships of care, mutual belonging, and responsibility to a shared community. This ethic of care and responsibility forms a crucial part of the foundation for building public life and public democracy.

CHAPTER 7

Curriculum and Pedagogy in
Two Democratic High Schools

School structure and organization can play key roles in nurturing
relationships that promote student engagement in programs of public democratic education. However, to the extent that students are
engaged in a democratic school's programs, the content of those
programs, that is, the curriculum and the teaching approaches used,
becomes central to students' experiences of democratic education.
The curriculum and pedagogy of the two democratic schools in this
study must therefore be examined closely, to determine how they
might contribute to the development of public democratic values
and capacities in young people.

Uptown High School Curriculum and Teaching

Uptown High School's curriculum is dramatically different in design
from the curriculum of a traditional high school. It is therefore
important to offer a fairly detailed description before discussing the
degree to which UHS's curriculum and teaching approaches encourage student engagement and preparation for public democratic
citizenship.

UHS Lower and Middle Section Curriculum and Pedagogy

Uptown High School does not attempt to be a "comprehensive" high school, in the sense of offering the full range of courses and electives that are found at most traditional high schools. UHS's Lower and Middle Section curriculum is built around a core of two interdisciplinary courses: humanities (which includes literature and social studies/history) and mathematics/science. These courses are taught in two-hour blocks, one in the morning and the other in the afternoon. Around these core curriculum blocks are built foreign language classes (taught from 8–9 a.m.), advisory classes, and electives in music, studio art, dance, sports and computer (taught at mid-day or from 3–5 p.m.). The two-hour time periods allow for in-depth exploration of curriculum themes through a variety of means. There are fewer of the disjointed shifts in focus that arise in most schools, where a bell rings every forty minutes to tell everyone to drop whatever they're doing or thinking and move on to the next class.

Lower and Middle Section Humanities/Social Studies

In humanities/social studies, four main curriculum themes are studied, one for each year for grades 7–10. Each year is made up of three trimesters. Classes study the year's overall curriculum theme from a different perspective each trimester. These themes were developed by a humanities/social studies teaching team. Materials and approaches to teaching these themes are constantly updated and developed by the teaching team.

Themes for the Lower Section (grades seven and eight) are The Peopling of America: The discovery, exploration, and settling of the North American continent; and Power: The emergence of contemporary political issues with a focus on U.S. history. Themes for the Middle Section (grades nine and ten) are Justice: comparative systems of law and government; and Non-European Traditions: stability and change in selected Asian, Central American, and African states.[1]

Each trimester, students work to complete a formal series of assignments—an exhibition—related to the curriculum theme. These

---

1. Uptown High School curriculum document.

assignments involve reading, research, literary analysis, creative writing, dramatizations of scenes of literary, historical or other significance, quizzes, and art work. Students work on these assignments individually and in groups throughout the term, doing multiple drafts and refining their work as they go. Final work on all assignments is due at the end of the trimester.

Students have the option of doing exhibition assignments at one of two levels: the "competency" level or the "advanced" level. Both competent and advanced level assignments deal with the same themes, issues, essential questions, and so on. The advanced level simply demands a higher complexity of work. In consultation with the teacher and parents, students decide at which level they wish to work on an exhibition. This is intended to be a flexible mechanism, so that students can work at their own ability and interest levels.

Lower and Middle Section Math/Science

The Lower and Middle Section math and science program stresses the importance of dealing with math and science concepts in a holistic manner that focuses on investigation, hypothesis formation, and hypothesis testing.[2] The concern is not to find single-answer solutions, but rather to develop a thought process for exploring math and science ideas and themes. Mathematical tools and practices such as graphs, equations, and computation are used to study the physical and the social world.

For math, there are three main curriculum themes:

1. How do I measure?
2. What does it mean to count?
3. Where am I and how did I get here?

These questions are meant to present opportunities to explore basic arithmetic, algebraic, and geometric ideas, as well as graphing. The third question is a metaphor that leads to working with issues of location and direction (plotting positions and paths on a plane), velocity, transportation costs (questions of value), and so forth.

For science, the curriculum themes are the following:

---

2. Interview with Robert Selig, math/science curriculum team leader, 23 May 1990.

Lower Section—How do we affect and improve the quality of life? This is a biology/natural sciences theme which looks at living organisms.

Middle Section—How do things change? This is a physical science theme that examines systems of objects and how they move relative to each other. It involves figuring out where things are and predicting where they'll be, using major notions of energy, conservation, velocity, momentum, etc.

Whenever possible, math concepts and procedures are taught in the context of their use in describing science phenomena and solving science problems. However, when necessary, certain aspects of math are taught and practiced apart from ongoing class science work.

There are two kinds of tasks that students are expected to master in the Lower and Middle Section math/science curriculum. The first involves process skills such as collecting and organizing data. For example, students might observe an object in motion. Then they would gather data on its velocity, direction, and so on, and perhaps draw a graph from it. Based on the data, students would then make the jump to the second type of tasks. This second kind of tasks gets to the essence of the math/science idea: drawing generalizable conclusions about the behavior of the object.[3]

Uptown H.S. mathematics and science teachers strive to develop projects that tie arithmetic or computational skills to larger math and science ideas. Computational skills are not handled separately, as a prerequisite to higher-order math and science ideas. Because traditional approaches to math and science instruction, by contrast, do treat computational skills as prerequisites to higher-order ideas, they tend to "lead to exclusion of people of color and of women."[4] This is because of the tendency for those groups to have relatively lower levels of computational training and skills. With the Uptown H.S. approach, students who are weaker in arithmetic skills are not penalized and excluded from working with higher-order math and science ideas, as they would be in a standard math or science program.

---

3. Ibid.
4. Ibid.

As in humanities/social studies, exhibition assignments designed by the math/science teaching team set the tasks through which math/science study is conducted. Student exhibitions are the concrete products of students' ongoing work in math and science. Students generally present their exhibitions orally to the teacher, or if they wish, to the class as a whole. They also hand them in in written form. The fact that students have to write up their exhibition reports, and then present them orally as well, raises the level of their expected mastery of the exhibition material.

Community Service

In addition to the academic curriculum, Lower and Middle Section students also work one morning (two to three hours) a week in a school/community service program. This program offers students their choice of placements with local schools, non-profit organizations, or businesses. In their community service placements, students do meaningful, supervised work that provides a service to others.

Through the community service program, over the four years of the Lower and Middle Sections, students get experience in a variety of fields in different institutional settings. They help out in elementary school classrooms; do office work in public service agencies; work on special projects in local museums; give tours of their own school to outside visitors; and so forth. As one example, a Middle Section student I ran into once at lunch time at a cheap Chinese restaurant near the school told me he was just returning from his community service work at a local museum of Latino culture. He and a classmate had worked there for the first trimester, and had decided to continue there for the present trimester.

> I asked him about community service. He said he worked helping the museum get ready for the Three Kings Parade (January 6). They worked reinforcing the parade floats, working on costumes, etc. The parade down the Avenue went well. People had also donated money with which presents were bought for kids. People dressed up as the Three Kings and went visiting kids in hospitals and giving them gifts. (Field notes, 22 February 1990.)

Students keep journal notes on their community service experiences, and at the end of each trimester, they write reports/critiques of their experiences. Supervisors, in turn, evaluate the students.[5] The community service program is intended to allow students to "contribute to [their] community," while they "develop a sense of responsibility toward others, acquire useful skills, learn about adult occupations, and participate in increasingly more responsible and complex tasks."[6]

Assessment and Family Conferences

Assessment of student progress and work is an ongoing process. Teachers assess student progress through observations of individual class work and student group work; conferences with individual students; and evaluation of group presentations, written essay drafts, and completed exhibitions. It is an observation-coaching process focused on both work in progress and final products.

At the end of each trimester, after exhibitions are completed and evaluated, teachers prepare narrative reports evaluating student progress over the trimester. Subject area and community service reports are compiled into a comprehensive report for each student. These become the basis for a discussion, in a family conference, of the student's progress and work.

After students and parents read the trimester report, they meet with the student's advisor for about forty minutes to discuss it. If the advisor feels that the conference would benefit from the involvement of any of the student's subject area teachers, this is arranged. The student's presence in the conference eliminates some of the confusion that can arise when the teacher, parents, and student have different understandings of what is going on in the student's work. Differences of this type can be resolved through face-to-face interaction among the parties. The conference process brings student, parents, and advisor together to identify that student's strengths and problem areas, and to decide on appropriate next steps to facilitate student growth. The family conferences provide another mechanism

---

5. Uptown High School curriculum document.
6. Uptown High School pamphlet.

for helping Uptown H.S. personalize the teaching and learning process.

The Upper Section Program and Curriculum[7]

At the end of tenth grade, if students have successfully completed all Middle Section courses and community service, and passed their second-language proficiency test and their state competency test in math, they enter the Upper Section. When a student enters the Upper Section, the student's advisor organizes a Graduation Committee which will have responsibility for evaluating the student's work and making a recommendation to the full faculty on the student's readiness to graduate. The Graduation Committee is made up of the advisor, another faculty member, a family member or other adult of the student's choosing, and an appointed tenth-grade student.

The defining task of the Upper Section is for students to complete portfolios of work that demonstrate mastery in fourteen required areas. Portfolios can take many different forms. Depending on the portfolio area, the specific topic students choose, and their own strengths and talents, students can submit written essays or art work, do dramatic presentations or readings, create videos or multimedia projects. Although students will be evaluated on their individual achievements, they may do part or all of a given portfolio project as a collaborative endeavor. Also, if done properly, one portfolio project can be used to cover more than one required portfolio area.

Although some of the portfolio projects may come out of work that students have begun in the Lower or Middle Sections, most of them are developed directly from the work students do in the Upper Section. Student work is done in connection with the five major organizing components of the Upper Section. These components include:

1. Regular Uptown H.S. course work. Students take courses either at Uptown H.S., or by arrangement with local colleges, on a tuition-free basis. During the spring 1991 semester, Upper Section students were enrolled in some thirty-three courses—twenty-one at Uptown H.S. and twelve at

---

7. Much of the following discussion of UHS's Upper Section is based on program descriptions in the 1991 Uptown High School Handbook.

cooperating colleges or technical schools.[8] These included such courses as geometry, pre-calculus, chemistry, physiology, short story, civil rights, geography, Second World War, sociology, video, internship seminar, computer design and maintenance, and construction trades.

2. Two Uptown H.S. college seminars. These are courses designed jointly by Uptown H.S. and local college faculty, taken on college campuses, aimed at providing students with a broad understanding of some of the major influences on the formation of our civilization.

3. Internships/Apprenticeships. All U.H.S. students must complete a one-semester part-time internship or a more intensive full-time summer apprenticeship in a selected job placement. This is intended to provide students with a fuller understanding of a chosen field of work which they may wish to consider as a career option.

4. Advisory/Independent Study. The advisory class takes on an expanded role in the Upper Section. Not only does it serve as a place where students explore personal, health, social and other issues, it also becomes a support group for students as they work on their portfolio projects. In addition, the advisor can become a supervisor for an independent study project, if a student chooses to do one for a portfolio project.

5. Post-Graduation Planning. During the first semester of the Upper Section, students work with their graduation committees to develop a tentative post-graduation plan. The plan, which is revised periodically as students adjust their thinking about their futures, includes short-term and long-term goals. Students take a series of concrete steps to implement their plans as they move through the Upper Section such as preparing resumes, investigating colleges or career training programs, preparing for required entrance exams, setting up college or job interviews, etc.[9]

---

8. "Graduating from Uptown H.S.: Comments by Maria Landon," a one-page assessment of Upper Section student progress and planning for graduation, and life after graduation. Fall 1990.

9. Uptown H.S. Handbook.

Through all the above means, students go about creating their graduation portfolios. The fourteen portfolio areas are the following:

1. Post-Graduate Plan
2. Autobiography
3. School/Community Service and Internship
4. Ethics and Social Issues
5. Fine Arts/Aesthetics
6. Practical Skills
7. Media
8. Geography
9. Second Language
10. Science/Technology*
11. Math*
12. History*
13. Literature*
14. Physical Challenge

(*Science, Math, History and Literature, along with three other portfolios of the student's choice, must be done as major presentations which are graded. Students can opt to have other portfolio items evaluated on a pass/fail basis.)

In addition, each student must choose one portfolio item and expand and develop it into a Final Senior Project. This should be a project in an area in which the student has particular talents, interests or knowledge. It is graded as both a regular portfolio item, and under more demanding criteria, as a Final Senior Project.

As this description of its organization and curriculum indicates, Uptown H.S. offers students a complex, expansive, and innovative set of educational experiences, quite unlike those available at a traditional comprehensive high school. However, it is only by examining the UHS curriculum closely, through the analytical framework developed in part I of this book, that one can see more clearly some of the specific ways in which UHS's curriculum offers opportunities for engaging students and encouraging their development as public democratic citizens.

Student Engagement at UHS: Intrinsic Interest, Real-World Meaning, and Student Ownership

When one examines the curriculum themes of UHS's Lower and Middle Sections, it is clear that they encourage student engagement. They are meaningful not only as academic themes, but they have meaning in the real world outside of school as well. For example, the Humanities themes of Peopling, Power, Justice, and Non-European Traditions all present a multitude of opportunities for making powerful connections with contemporary social issues and ideas. The study of issues of social justice and the discussion of critical public issues are also two of the ideal school practices for developing young people's public democratic values and attributes. The Math/Science themes are also thoroughly grounded in real world physical and social phenomena and for that reason are likely to encourage student engagement.

Student exhibitions, and to an even greater extent, Upper Section student portfolios, present opportunities for students to become engaged in doing work which is intrinsically interesting, and which gives them a sense of ownership. Within each set of exhibition tasks, as well as among the fourteen Upper Section portfolio projects, students can choose to focus their energies and efforts in any of a wide range of ways. Although students must do a certain minimum level of work in all the exhibition and portfolio areas, they can give maximum effort in areas in which they have particular personal interests, skills, or talents. Such multifaceted learning projects, incidentally, also allow students to best apply their different "intelligences" to their studies.[10]

The study of the specific content and the intellectual rigor applied to the completion of exhibition and portfolio projects also helps students develop several of the capacities necessary for public democratic participation. Students are encouraged to develop clear oral and written expression of their ideas; facility in working collaboratively with others; skills in doing research, to enable them to learn more about any issue that arises; knowledge of constitutional rights and political processes; and an understanding of some of the connections among public issues to each other and to issues in the past.

The community service and internship programs are also likely to engage students. Students participating in these programs enjoy a degree of choice (ownership) so they can explore their own interests, and opportunities to do real work in the world (real world meaning). Many of the community service placements also give

---

10. Howard Gardner, *Frames of Mind* (New York: Basic Books, 1983).

students the experience of making a positive contribution to their community, which may contribute to their development of an ethic of care and responsibility.

Finally, the "habits of mind" approach which permeates curriculum and teaching at UHS, encourages students constantly to examine and evaluate critically everything they see in the world. This habit of critically examining the social world is also a key attribute needed for public democratic citizenship.

Metropolitan High School Curriculum and Teaching

The curriculum at Metropolitan High School is also quite different from that of a traditional comprehensive high school. In traditional Metro City academic high school classes, the curriculum is largely dictated by the material students will be expected to know on the state competency exams. Classes at Metropolitan H.S., on the other hand, are not geared to the state competency tests. They are not designed to "cover" all the material mandated by the state curriculum. Metropolitan H.S. believes in depth and process, rather than coverage. As co-director Michael Bell sees it,

> We're quite prepared to have our kids, who are capable of passing the state competency test, pass it with a 70 instead of a 99, and know how to do science [for example], rather than simply know how to take a science test.[11]

Metropolitan H.S. also tries to be as flexible as possible in order to serve the diverse needs of its unique student body. Students come to Metropolitan from other schools which for a variety of reasons, they rejected, and for the most part, stopped attending. They arrive with varying levels of academic skills and knowledge, depending on what they were able to learn before they stopped going to classes at their previous schools. The MHS staff works together to plan what courses to offer to meet students' needs. What is emphasized in any given course is also influenced by staff discussion of what students need.

---

11. Interview with Michael Bell, 2 July 1991.

At the time of my research at Metropolitan H.S., a student's graduation depended in part on his/her completion of a required number of academic credits, much as it would in a traditional high school. However, the school at that time was beginning to institute a proficiency-based set of graduation requirements, involving some type of portfolio system. Metropolitan H.S. has begun moving away from the credit system altogether, in favor of this portfolio graduation requirement.[12]

The Metropolitan H.S. curriculum is designed to get students to do research, to investigate issues through various sources, to draw conclusions and take positions on the issues. At the beginning of every semester, students do intensive, 3–4-week group inquiry studies on different aspects of assigned research themes. In February 1991, when I began my observations at MHS, I saw the students in action on such a research project.

The students worked in small research teams, each under the guidance of a teacher, investigating the theme of community. Different groups did projects on such topics as African-American and Latino communities; utopian communities; housing projects as communities; gay and lesbian religious communities; and the influence of high-profile political figures such as Jesse Jackson and Al Sharpton, as well as popular rap artists, in the communities of their followers. Students investigated questions such as: "What is a community? Do these groups constitute communities? What would make them communities?"

Teachers encouraged and guided their students to tap some of the vast resources of Metro City in doing their research. Students used special public library collections and interviewed activists, experts, and people with direct experience in students' research areas. At the end of the month, students wrote 15–20-page papers based on their research. This type of intensive research project is used as a kick-off to every new semester, to get new students "baptized" into inquiry-based learning, and to get continuing students refocused on the work at hand.

---

12. Co-director Karen Meese, in a phone conversation, 15 November 1992. In a few cases, if students have a special need to move on without completing all the graduation requirements, MHS staff may encourage them to take the G.E.D. test. But Metropolitan H.S. staff still continue to provide academic support and counseling to help such students prepare for and get into college.

After the semester-opening research project, students choose classes and begin to settle into them. During my period of observation at the school, classes offered included such courses as Adolescent Issues, Spanish, French, Work and Workers, Supreme Court, African and Latin American Literature, Media Investigation, Action Research, Chemistry, Calculus, American History, Sexist Society?, Politics of Money, Novels, Evolution, Studio Art, Video, and so on. A few of these classes are taught by special arrangement by college faculty at their colleges. The classes I observed were Action Research, Politics of Money, Sexist Society?, American History, and Novels. These were all taught by regular Metropolitan H.S. faculty, with classes taking place in the school, except when special trips were taken in connection with the course of study. (In the Action Research class, there were almost weekly trips to meet with educational advocates, activists and writers, to attend public forums, etc.)

In-class work is centered on discussion and debate of a variety of issues. Students often work in pairs or small groups to gather evidence from readings and organize their arguments. They also use evidence they have gathered through class readings or through their own research to argue their points of view.

Most classes are 50–55 minutes long. However, two afternoons a week are organized into two-period blocks of time to allow for more in-depth exploration of a topic of study, or for trips outside the school, or other kinds of plans that aren't easily limited to 50 or 55 minute periods. A third afternoon each week, from 12:15 on, is blocked out for students to participate in their community-service work.

Community Service placements are set up by the Metropolitan H.S. staff. They try to arrange a wide variety of placements, in lawyer's offices, schools, health centers, social services such as drug treatment programs, nursing homes, and so on. Students, in consultation with staff, choose from the list of possible placements. If they are dissatisfied with the available placements, or if they have a special interest that they would like to pursue, students can work with a staff person or on their own to try to set up a community-service placement that better suits them.

Community Service at Metropolitan H.S. serves several objectives. It puts students in a position to "have a role in the wider community"[13] outside of school, and to make a contribution to that community. It also offers students a chance, over the course of their high school experience, to get a sense of the variety of adult roles in their community. Community service can also allow students to explore a particular interest they may have, and see whether it holds up under the scrutiny of direct experience. Finally, staff members can guide students to explore areas through community service in which they feel the students will be interested, but which the students might never consider otherwise. In this sense, community service provides students with an opportunity "to stick their noses into different aspects of life."[14]

Student Engagement at MHS: Intrinsic Interest, Real-World Meaning, and Student Ownership

The research/inquiry focus of the MHS curriculum creates a learning environment in the school that is highly conducive to student engagement in activities that promote students' development as public democratic citizens. This is apparent in a number of aspects of MHS's curriculum and teaching approaches. For example, the themes students investigate in their semester-opening intensive research projects and in their classes, are consciously designed to open up a broad range of vital, and sometimes controversial, real-world issues, which possess high intrinsic interest for the students. Since students choose individual and small-group research topics within overall research and class themes, they also gain a large measure of ownership over the research process. In addition, MHS's practice of encouraging students to utilize out-of-school resources in their intensive research projects and in their regular classwork infuses their work with a sense of real-world meaning and importance.

Since MHS classes are specifically designed by teachers with students' interests and needs in mind, they are likely to hold intrinsic interest for students. Students' ability to choose their classes also adds to their sense of ownership of the learning process.

---

13. Interview with Michael Bell, 2 July 1991.
14. Ibid.

There are also a number of ways in which the MHS curriculum directly encourages students to develop public democratic values, attributes, and capacities. For example, students' work in research project teams, as well as regular group work in classes, provides opportunities for exploring their interdependence with their peers. Research themes such as the one on community also directly encourage students to examine questions of people's interdependence in different kinds of social groups. The focus of MHS classes around discussion and debate of public issues offers another way to encourage students' development of public democratic habits and capacities.

The school's inquiry learning orientation continually leads students into a critical examination of social reality, and contributes to their development of a critical/analytical social outlook. The inquiry approach also offers students multiple opportunities to develop a number of the capacities necessary for public democratic citizenship. Specifically, this approach constantly involves students in analysis of written and spoken language, in the context of exploring the complexities of major public issues. It forces students to express their ideas and arguments clearly, both orally and in writing. The inquiry approach turns the learning process over to students, to work independently and in small groups. Students thus gain facility in both independent and collaborative work, investigating ideas and issues. These abilities provide students with the foundation they will need to understand and respond to public issues they confront in the future.

CHAPTER 8

Promoting Public Democratic Citizenship

Student Responses to School Programs

A deeper understanding of the complexities of public democratic education at Uptown and Metropolitan High Schools can be gained by examining two exemplary classes, one in each school. Examining these two classes leads to important insights about students' responses to the overall organization and practices of the two schools.

MHS: Action Research Class

Karen Meese taught a class called Action Research at Metropolitan High School. In this class, students spent an entire term investigating a current social issue, and developing a class project that would attempt to make a public impact on the issue. During the spring term of 1991, the issue they investigated was the proposed set of cutbacks in aid to Metro City public education. Karen Meese organized the course around current newspaper and journal readings on important educational concerns in Metro City, the nation, and the world. She also set up a number of class meetings around the city for interviews and discussions with education experts, activists, board of education officials, and others.

One particular class I observed gives a taste of what students experienced in this course. The class went to visit a local newspaper writer, Sally Karas, who had recently done an article for the *Metro City Chronicle* contrasting Japanese and American education. The students were given copies of her article to read before the meeting, as well as an assignment to prepare two interview questions in advance and to take notes during the discussion. The following excerpts from my field notes provide a sense of how the meeting went.

[The setting was not very conducive to discussion. Sally Karas took us all up to the *Metro City Chronicle* cafeteria to have lunch. However, the tables weren't big enough for everyone to sit around one, and several of us had to pull up chairs from other tables to form an outside circle around those seated at the table. The cafeteria was quite crowded and noisy. Neither Sally Karas', nor most of the students' voices carried very well. So most questions, answers and comments had to be repeated in order to be heard at both ends of the table. Nevertheless, most students did pay close attention and participate in the discussion. Only in the last few minutes of the hour-long discussion did a couple of students at my end of the table seem to lose interest.]

[Discussion begins with student comments/questions. Mitch says something about Japanese students studying so much that they're all nerds and freaks. Other students respond that he's just judging them by his standards. Other Japanese students don't consider good students or those who study a lot to be nerds. The culture respects such students.]

Sally Karas (SK): Almost everyone, maybe 98% of Japanese students, graduate high school. Everyone learns enough to be literate and to use numbers. . . . They know that if they work hard they'll get good jobs. . . .

Jane: But you're acting as if it's all or nothing. Either they work hard and get great jobs or they don't and they're total failures. There must be hairdressers in Japan, and places like MacDonald's where people work. . . .

SK: That's right. But they learn enough in high school or even in junior high school to function in their jobs. When I was in Japan,

I had a hairdresser who I became friends with. He had actually dropped out of high school. But he had learned enough in junior high school to be able to keep records for his business, to run the business.

Michael: Do kids enjoy school in Japan? What's it like?

SK: In the early grades, school is very creative. Then in junior high school and high school it gets very competitive, very rote, a lot of memorizing. . . .

Mary: But it's different in Japan. Home and school work closely together [to support education].

SK: Yes. Families are very involved in the student's education. . . . But I don't necessarily think that everything's perfect with the Japanese approach to education. There is too much pressure too early on the kids. . . .

Jane: So what's your idea of a perfect education system?

SK: Something in the middle. There it's too much pressure. Here it's too little. Kids should learn enough to get along and to want to learn new things.

Karen Meese: What are classes like [in Japan]?

SK: A lot of lecture. Not much discussion. Big classes—30 to 40 students in a class. . . .

Jose: Maybe they realize if they work hard for now, they'll have it made. . . .

Karen Meese: [Talks about raising the ante: demanding more work from students in American schools].

Ron: But if you raise the ante, it might just blow up in your face. More might drop out. If now 15 percent drop out, then 30 to 40 percent might drop out.

Steve: I think if you want more people to pass high school, you have to make it easier. Making it harder won't work. [A lot of kids just won't do it.]

SK: I think that's bad! I have to say I think that's bad, what you're saying.

Melissa: What? Make it easier? But we're already way behind other countries!

Karen Meese: That's right. Sally, what's the unemployment rate in Japan?

SK: Very low. Almost none.

Karen Meese: And you know, right here in Metro City at least 1 of every 10 people is out of work. And the standard of living hasn't gone up since 1973! Do you know what that means? We're not keeping up. . . .

Michelle: Yeah, it's the economy. It's not doing too well.

[Then there was discussion about whether there are jobs available now. One student said there are jobs in MacDonald's. People can get jobs if they want one. Karen Meese replies that those jobs don't pay anything and they discuss that a bit. Then Karen and SK try to get students to say what would motivate them to work hard in school.]

SK: [Suggests the possibility of a national competency test that all graduating students would have to take.]

Karen Meese: What if we had a test, a national test that you all had to take? And when you went for a job, employers would ask, "Well, what did you get on the test? What was your score?" Would that make you want to work hard in school? Would that motivate you? You wouldn't necessarily like it. But would you work hard?

[A few say yes. Then one student says]: What would the test be testing for? Would it really mean anything? Would it have anything to do with the job you're applying for? A few people pick up on that issue, commenting on how tests often have little to do with what people can actually *do* with their knowledge.][1]

This class experience was quite valuable, on several levels. On one level it was a good opportunity for the students to make contact with the real world of a key Metro City business, the news

---

1. Field notes, 25 March 1996.

media. Students got the opportunity to go into the *Metro City Chronicle* building and have lunch with a *Chronicle* writer. They sat around a big table, eating lunch and talking about education with Sally Karas, asking her questions and sometimes challenging her answers. In this way they were able to demystify her and her profession, and see that she was a very normal person. By participating as equals in a discussion in which they shared their own ideas about education as much as they listened to Karas', they also raised themselves up to her level. Students were intentionally put in the position of being the questioners and commentators on Karas' ideas. This gave them a degree of control and ownership of the process, and made it an engaging and empowering experience.

On another level, the topic, education, held intrinsic interest for the students. Discussion built upon students' experience and knowledge of education, as well as their knowledge of the Metro City economic situation and job market. It also drew upon what they had recently read, including Karas' article. Not only was the situation real (interviewing a writer on her home ground), but the topic was one that connected directly to the students' reality. Moreover, it was also a topic of major importance in city and national politics, and in the media.

The whole process of the Action Research class also involved students in examining, discussing, debating, and writing about many of the major questions around the state of American education and its future. The process provides an excellent illustration of a set of educational practices organized into a course that encourages students to examine critically the social reality in which they live. It also gives them a great deal of practice in a number of the skills necessary for public democratic participation: active listening, analyzing written and spoken language, expressing their ideas in speech and in writing, and throughout, working collaboratively with their peers. They also examine some of the linkages between educational issues and others (economic, political, cultural).

These activities contribute to the development of the values, attributes, and capacities necessary for public democratic citizenship. Working in collaborative groups reinforces feelings of interdependence among students, which is one of the first steps toward building an ethic of care and responsibility. Since class research is focused on public issues and action, it strengthens students' sense of the importance of public life and public action. Finally, the nature of the research, which constantly asks students to examine their own ideas about education and educational policy, and to examine and challenge the ideas of others, leads to a critical, analytical social outlook.

It should be noted that the Action Research class is not unique at Metropolitan H.S. in its high level of intrinsic interest for students, the sense that it gives students of ownership over their work, and the way it deals with real-world issues. Many classes demonstrated these characteristics and appeared to be highly engaging to students.[2]

The point that schoolwork at Metropolitan H.S. deals with real-world issues was also made by two students one day over lunch. After talking with each of them for a short while, I asked whether they thought Metropolitan H.S. was preparing them for life after high school. Here's how they responded:

Ann [African-American]: Yes, because we talk about real-life things. Also, community service, that's real-life stuff. . . .

Karen [African-American]: I guess so. Because they deal with real things here. Like you were here in American History class today, right?

[She refers to an emotional, but reasoned discussion comparing the relative strengths and internal unity of African-American communities and Jewish communities and how that may or may not affect the ability of members of those communities to be successful in life.]

In other schools they'd try to play that down. They wouldn't want to talk about it in class. But here we can talk about it.[3]

During one of the focus group discussions I ran, another student made the point even more strongly.

John [African-American]: Something that stands out to me is history. . . . At one time, Karen taught an "Eyes on the Prize" class.

---

2. I will go into more detail later about students' sense of ownership and control in decisions that affect their day-to-day experience of school life.
3. Field notes 16 April 1991.

That was sort of a history class dealing with the civil rights movement in the United States. And that stood out, because that's been something that's been dear to me as a person in this community [the African-American community]. But also just by the way that she did it, and being that she had a lot of first-person accounts, you know, the people who we interviewed, and people who we talked to. And that made it just much [more] real, than always looking to a book all the time.

And lots of the educational process in Metropolitan H.S. is such that you can actually take it beyond a school. You know what I'm saying? *This affects life....* I think just about every class in Metropolitan, whether direct or indirect, has an effect on your life. You know, after high school, and after college, and after whatever ... every class, whether direct or indirect, somehow will have an effect.

UHS: Video Documentary Class

At Uptown H.S., too, many of the classes and much student work were characterized by high levels of intrinsic interest for students, real-world meaning, and some degree of student ownership and control. The video documentary class in the Upper Section is one class that combined these elements to create a highly engaging experience for students. During the first half of the semester students learned the video production process—from use of cameras and lighting and sound equipment to editing a final product—by doing a couple of small video projects based in the school. The class I observed had done short documentaries on how Upper Section advanced students feel about their upcoming graduation; and about how Uptown H.S. students and staff feel about a school dress code rule, the "no hats" rule.

The second half of the term was devoted to creating students' semester projects. The semester project had to be a documentary on a social issue that involved some sort of debate or controversy. The spring, 1991 semester topic was rap music: its effects on young people, whether there should be censorship of obscene lyrics, sexism in rap, and whether rap artists have a responsibility to "send out positive messages."

Kevin Johnson, the video teacher, offered me some of his thoughts on the project and what he wanted students to get out of it.

> *Kevin*: Students choose the project topic. It's a democratic process. I didn't think this rap topic was the best one, but that's what they wanted to do. And it has some real possibilities. . . . Last semester they did a project on media coverage of the Persian Gulf War. There was so much research involved before actually getting out there and interviewing and videotaping. This time I want to have them use people as resources. I want them to talk with experts and learn from them. That way they can get right out and start taping interviews.

> *DS*: Oh, so this isn't just going to be a public opinion kind of thing?

> *Kevin*: No. I think there's a danger in doing that, going out and taping just anyone's opinion. I want this to be a documentary. I want them to talk with experts and really present some thoughtful ideas. Not that I want them to think students and regular people don't have anything to say. But I want them to learn that there are people out there who have really thought about this a lot, and worked on it. They'll be interviewing people like [a well-known writer for a local newspaper, who's written a lot on rap music]. And maybe members of the Parents' Music Resource Center. . . .[4] I want them to learn to use people as resources.[5]

On the first day I observed the video class, they were just getting started on video-taping. Although the intention was to solicit the views of "experts" on rap music and its influence on young people, the students felt that they should start with interviews of their fellow students. They developed the following four-question interview guide to use with Uptown H.S. students:

1. What kind of influence does rap music have on you or on people in general?

---

4. This refers to the group that created and publicized a warning label system for recordings that have sexually explicit lyrics. This group was organized under the leadership of Tipper Gore, wife of Vice-President Al Gore.

5. Field notes, 11 April 1991.

2. Do you think musicians have the responsibility to send out positive messages?
3. What kind of thoughts run through your mind when you listen to songs with explicit lyrics? Should these lyrics be allowed?
4. Do you think songs like "Pimpin' Ain't Easy" affect the way women are treated?

The class divided into two video crews, got their equipment together and headed out into the halls. I followed one crew of five, with another two students coming late from other meetings to join them. Students took turns doing the three different roles on the interview crew—interviewer (holding microphone), camera person, and sound monitor (wearing earphones). I have excerpted below parts of some of the answers students gave to the interview questions.

[Q1: On influence of rap music]

Tammie [African-American female]: Yes. It has an influence, mostly on guys. They see how rappers dress and they wanna dress like them. . . .

[Q3: Should explicit lyrics be allowed?]

Tammie: [She talks about the labels they now put on tapes, records, and CDs if they are judged to be too explicit.] But it doesn't stop anybody from buying them. It probably just makes them more interested.

[Q4: Does "Pimpin' Ain't Easy" affect treatment of women?]

Tammie: I think a lot of factors contribute to the way guys treat women. It's not rap music that makes them treat women bad [or good]. It's the way they're brought up.

[Q2: Do musicians have responsibility to send out positive messages?]

Mark [African-American male]: Yeah, because they might influence people.

[Q3: Should explicit lyrics be allowed?]

Mark: I guess. It's all about freedom of speech. . . .

[Q1: On influence of rap music]

Andrew [White male]: Well, I write songs. So I think it influences you.

[Q2: Do musicians have responsibility to send out positive messages?]

Andrew: I think musicians should send out a message, but not necessarily a positive one. . . .

[Q4: Does "Pimpin' Ain't Easy" affect treatment of women?]

Andrew: I personally wouldn't write lyrics that are degrading. But if a person is going to go out and rape someone after hearing a song, they're already screwed up.

[Q1: On influence of rap music]

Kevin (African-American male]: Yeah, some. There are different kinds of artists. Some talk about girls, some are political. I listen to all kinds. . . .

[Q2: Do musicians have responsibility to send out positive messages?]

Kevin: Yes. Some use it as a tool to get a point across.

[Q3: Should explicit lyrics be allowed?]

Kevin: You mean pertaining to the First Amendment? Well, some kids are too young. They hear about 2 Live Crew and they don't know what they're about. But they hear about them. So they go out and buy the tape.

[Q4: Does "Pimpin' Ain't Easy" affect treatment of women?

Kevin: Myself, it doesn't affect me. I already have my mind made up.

[Q3: Should explicit lyrics be allowed?]

Eduardo [Latino male]: Well, the Constitution says free speech is allowed. So they should be able to say what they want.

[Q4: Does "Pimpin' Ain't Easy" affect treatment of women?

Eduardo: Yeah, I think it does. I think it degrades them. Like [gives name of a popular rapper], he says degrading things about women on one side. But on the other side he says "upgrade the race." It's a contradiction.[6]

It is clear that the video documentary class at Uptown H.S. fulfills three of the characteristics that encourage young people to become engaged in their school life. In focusing on the influence of rap music on young people, it deals with issues that are meaningful in the real world, and indeed are connected to students' own experience and knowledge as participants in urban youth culture. The semester video project is also of great interest to the students, for in fact it was selected by them. Their ability to choose the topic, to decide whom to interview, develop interview questions, and retain ultimate editorial control over the final product, all contribute to a strong sense of ownership of the video project.

The students were in fact engaged in the project, at least on the days when I observed. For example, on the day they interviewed other Uptown H.S. students, each student participated in some phase of the interviewing process, as well as in a technical critique session that took place back in the classroom during the last half hour of the class.

In observing the student video crews roam the school's halls in search of interview subjects, another type of ownership was apparent. The students seemed to "own" the halls and rooms of the school. They were totally at ease walking in and out of open classrooms (where classes were not going on), down the corridors, stopping briefly to talk to fellow students who were out of their classes on breaks, in travel to the library, the bathroom, or some other destination, or perhaps on free periods. Teachers and staff members did not stop the student video teams, nor the other students for that matter, to ask for passes or for explanations of where they were "supposed to be," as is commonplace in other schools. And although the halls were not exactly quiet, they were also not particularly noisy or chaotic, and certainly did not feel in any way

---

6. Field notes, 11 April 1991.

threatening. I attribute this situation of "disorderly orderliness" to the school's small size, and to that combination of other organizational factors described earlier which lead to an overall sense of membership and safety in the school.

The semester project investigation of the influence of rap music on young people provides an excellent illustration of one of the ideal secondary school practices for nurturing democratic values and attributes in young people. It leads students into a critical examination of the social reality in which they live. The fact that the students chose this topic shows that they are already beginning to develop a critical social outlook, an essential attribute of citizens in a public democracy.

The questions students developed for interviewing their schoolmates place them, and the interviewees, face-to-face with several vital social issues. For example, the first question on the influence of rap music on students, and the fourth, on whether a particularly misogynistic song affects the way men treat women, both seek to examine the power of popular culture in society. The second question, whether musicians have a responsibility to send out positive messages, raises the issue of one's responsibility to a community or society. This can lead, in turn, to consideration of the need for an ethic of care and responsibility, a necessary foundation of public democratic citizenship. The third question, whether explicit or obscene lyrics should be allowed, opens up the whole issue of the relationship between individual freedom of expression and the common or social good, and the extent or limits of social power to enforce a perceived social good.

The answers students gave to these questions are also worth examining, even though they are by no means a scientific sample of the views of Uptown H.S. students. The three affirmative answers to question 1 point to at least some recognition among Uptown H.S. students that popular culture may have an influence on social life. Yet this is balanced by their responses to the fourth question, which demonstrate some understanding of the complexity of this relationship. The four negative answers to the question about the effect of a song on the treatment of women, all indicate that these students do not see a simplistic cause-and-effect relationship between a particular song and men's attitudes toward women. Even Eduardo's positive answer doesn't claim that the song causes men to act in a certain way. He simply says the song degrades women, an assumption made by all the respondents. The implication of all their answers is that they feel that the influence of popular culture works as one part of a complex set of forces to influence individual actions.

Student answers to the second question offer no clear pattern, with two saying musicians do have a responsibility to produce positive messages, and one saying they don't, while the answers of the other two students were not recorded. However, student responses to the third question on whether explicit lyrics should be allowed are revealing, but not for the specific positions the students took. Of the four whose answers I have recorded, three students made specific reference to the question's connection to the Constitution, the First Amendment, or freedom of speech. I was impressed by the fact that they did not simply say, "this is a free country," but that they had some awareness of the foundation in the Constitution of the specific freedom in question. Some knowledge of constitutional structures and protections is one of the minimal capacities necessary for public democratic citizenship.

The process of producing the video documentary projects is itself a valuable educational exercise for preparing young people for public citizenship. Doing group research on a public issue, identifying activists and experts on the issue, developing interview questions and conducting interviews, all offer students opportunities to analyze written, spoken, and image language, practice active listening skills, develop their ability to work collaboratively with others, and gain an understanding of the complexities of a major public issue. These are all capacities that are necessary for public democratic participation. In addition, the experience students get in the technical aspects of video production, from taping to editing to manipulation of the sound track (adding music, voice-overs, etc.) helps to demystify television for students. It contributes to a critical understanding among students of how professional documentaries and news reports are made, and the degree to which ideological and political decisions play a role at every step in the process. Once students gain this critical understanding of video production, they will never again view television news, documentaries, or interviews with passivity and naive acceptance.

The experiences students had in Kevin Johnson's video class seemed to embody many of the ideal organizational features and teaching practices that I have argued will lead to high levels of student engagement and the development in students of many of the values, attributes, and capacities necessary for public democratic citizenship. Because students chose their own project topics, and often interviewed the students and staff of Uptown H.S. in at least one part of their projects, the class also proved quite useful to me as a field researcher. The choice of topics served as a window into some of the issues students in the class considered important, while the interviews offered a forum for other students' views on these issues. An excellent example of how this worked can be seen in the story of the "No Hats" video.

"No Hats" Video

A couple of weeks after I observed the video class doing their initial interviews with students for the rap music project, I accompanied them on a bus trip to a record, tape, and CD store. The class was going to the music store to do video interviews with customers about their views of the warning label system for recordings with explicit lyrics.

On the bus going to the music store, I had the following conversation with Gail and Monica, two Upper Section students, Latina and African-American, respectively.

[I asked Gail and Monica about their first video project for this class. They told me there was one on the school's dress code—the "no hat" rule. Note: Uptown H. S. students are officially prohibited from wearing hats in the school building. My own impression is that the rule is inconsistently enforced.]

DS: I've never understood that rule. What's it for?

Gail: I don't know. I guess it's because—I don't know. You know, this is supposed to be such an alternative place and everything, but then they have the same rules as all the other schools. . . .

Monica: And they want us to protest and all. . . . [She tells of teachers urging students to go to a recent student demonstration against education cutbacks at City Hall. She points out the irony that teachers want students to be critical and to be activists, yet also want them to conform to what they see as a silly dress code.]

DS: What did you do for that video project?

Gail: We interviewed teachers and students about the hat rule.

DS: What did the teachers say?

Gail: Mostly that they don't like it either, but it's a rule.

DS: What did the students you interviewed say?

Gail: Against it! Nobody likes the rule.

[I asked if they ever protested anything in the school, against any school policies. They told me about one day when everybody wore hats to school as a protest. But nothing came of it.

Monica also mentioned a demonstration for outside lunch privileges for Middle Section students. But since they're in the Upper Section now it doesn't matter, because Upper Section students can eat lunch out of the building.][7]

This conversation provided several important pieces of information. First, there was a school issue (the "no hats" rule) that these students felt was so important that they chose it as a topic for their first short video documentary. Second, there was a student-made videotape that could provide me with a set of brief student and teacher interviews on the issue. Third, Monica's mention of the demonstration for outside lunch privileges for Middle Section students highlighted the importance of that issue, which had previously been brought to my attention by other students. Fourth, however happy they may have been with the school overall, Gail and Monica also harbored a certain frustration with the contradiction between what the school says it wants them to be outside of school—critical and active citizens—and what it seems to want them to be inside of school—acquiescent and passive students, at least when it comes to certain school rules.

To investigate the "no hat" rule issue further, I took my first opportunity to borrow the No Hats videotape from Kevin Johnson. Below are my notes from viewing the five-minute tape.

---

7. Field notes, 25 April 1991.

Narrator: [This video explores students' and teachers' views on the hat rule.] By the end of this video, you the people of Uptown H.S. should be able to determine whether the rule is a valid one.

African-American male student: I think the rule should be changed.

Mike [white teacher]: What do I think, personally? Probably it wouldn't matter to me.

Joe [African-American student interviewer, *wearing baseball cap*]: What is the big deal on guys and girls wearing hats in school?

Jean Summers [Upper Section director, African-American female]: I felt it was important because, especially young black males are often judged on the basis of how they look. And because in the larger society, wearing a hat inside of a building connotes respect or disrespect, you all needed to have some consciousness about that. To make yourselves consciously aware of that, one way would be to make you all take your hats off, so that it would be an automatic response or reflex when you go into other places, in which you want to make an impression, if you want to go on a job interview etc., etc.

[Cut to interview with African-American male student.]

Joe: I see you have the Jamaican colors on [referring to the green, yellow, and red baseball cap the student is wearing]. Is that to be cultural, I mean, why do you have your hat on? Are you doing this just to disobey the rules?

Ron: Well I'm one of those people you can call a rebel. I really don't feel that the rule is one that I want to follow, so I go against it. . . .

Joe: [Says something, cut off on tape, about getting together with other students to try to change the rule.]

Ron: Well, from my experience in this school, I see that a lot of rules cannot be changed no matter what people try to do, including students. I feel that there's no need for me to try to get together with other students and make a change because there will be no change. And being that I'm gonna be leaving quite soon, I'll just be a rebel for the rest of the time and continue to wear my hat. . . .

[In another interview Amy, an African-American female student says she doesn't think students should wear hats in school.]

Amy: Well honestly, as a growing up adult, teaching you, preparing you for life, guys shouldn't wear hats. It's like a general rule.... If you're going to be in a working environment, you have to learn how to follow rules and regulations.

Joe: Do you think that it should be different for a male and female? Should they both have to take their hats off inside?

Amy: Yeah. Both should have to take off their hats.... Everything should be equal for everybody....

[Note: Amy looks very much like a "growing up adult." She has a very put-together look, with her fashionable black pants suit, silver earrings, and a stylish red and black leather hat. Joe, the interviewer, is wearing a baseball cap. His friend, who stands next to him during the interview, also has a hat on.]

[The video ends with several cuts to students commenting on the no hat rule.]

Students: It sucks!
   Bullshit!
   Keep rockin' your hats!
   That's the nineties.
[Student grabs the mike from interviewer and says]:
   Yeah, for the 90s. 'Cause that's the only way we're gonna' change things around here.
[Then he turns and points right into the camera and shouts]:
   Suckers! Fresh! For '91!
[End of video.]

Based on my observations, as well as teacher and student comments about the hat rule, both in the video and in private conversations, it appears that the hat issue, silly as it might seem, serves as a window into a weakness in Uptown High School's program for public democratic education.

The two teachers seen in the video had differing views on the hat rule. The first indicated no personal investment in the no hat rule. The second did feel strongly enough about it that she made an effort to give a rationale for the rule. Yet the fact is, there was no strong commitment on the part of the faculty to enforce the hat rule consistently.

The number of students wearing hats in the video was no doubt a function of the "freedom of hats" sentiment of the video team. However, it is true that many, many students did wear hats regularly in the halls and even in classrooms. Teachers and the principal often asked students to remove their hats, and students usually complied. But often teachers failed to ask. And if they did ask, students tended to take their hats off for a while, and then put them back on later. Students were fighting a guerilla war of style against a dress code that had been imposed on them by the teaching staff. And although the teachers were not fully united in their resolve to win the war, they also did not want to give up the principle that they had the exclusive right to impose rules (with the noblest intentions) on their young charges, the students.

Maria Landon, the principal, was aware of this contradiction, and wanted it resolved. At a staff meeting in January 1990, she brought the issue to the teachers' attention.

[Maria Landon speaks on need to enforce rules about students not wearing hats and coats in class or in halls; no eating junk food in class; no gum; no Walkmen. Or else drop the rules. She thinks these policies are not being followed, and that it makes the school look bad.]

Maria: ... I'm not willing to write it up again in the Newsletter, nor any other regulation if staff aren't going to enforce it.

[Maria's proposal:] Form a student and parent committee to make rules on dress, junk food, etc.

[There's a staff discussion of the proposal. In a staff vote, *the proposal is defeated* by a large majority on the sense of the faculty that, as one person stated in the discussion]:

The staff assembly should be the highest authority in the school.

[It appears that teachers are not willing to delegate any of their rule-making authority to students and/or parents, even on an issue such as dress code.][8]

---

8. Field notes, 22 January 1990.

The crucial point here is this: *students had no institutionalized input into how the school was run.* In fact, a week after the staff vote against forming a parent/student rules committee, I was told by a teacher that there was no student government of any kind at Uptown H.S. As he explained it, "Helen [one of the teachers] tried to organize one with students last year, but no students turned out to a meeting. Since the administration wasn't too keen on the idea anyway, the idea died."[9] Thus students had no formal mechanism for making or influencing school rules and regulations at Uptown H.S.

The lack of formal channels of student influence had significant consequences for their early experiences of democracy. Student responses to their lack of input on the no hat rule illustrate this point.

Based on the video and on my observations and discussions with students, it seems that most Uptown H.S. students were against the no hat rule. According to Gail and Monica, they tried to organize against the rule by holding a one-day protest, for which everyone wore a hat to school. But nothing came of it. Since the students had no institutionalized power, and their attempt at creating organized, public power through protest seemed to fail, they fell back to a reliance on personal power—the power of individual resistance. This dynamic could hardly have been articulated more clearly than it was in Ron's statement in the video: "I feel that there's no need for me to try to get together with other students and make a change because there will be no change. . . . [So] I'll just be a rebel for the rest of the time and continue to wear my hat."

Individual resistance is an expression of a kind of power. But it is a power that is diffuse, spontaneous, and fleeting. And as Ron, Gail, and Monica's attitudes show us, resistance can take on a tone of frustrated resignation. I heard the same resigned tone echoed in the words of Annie, another student who had been active during the 1989–90 school year trying to organize Middle Section students to win out-of-school lunch privileges.

Annie: Maria [Landon] wrote us a letter [in the *Newsletter*] that basically said, "Forget it. There's no way you're going to get this. So you might as well give up and stop protesting."[10] You'd think

---

9. Field Notes, 29 January 1990.

10. I actually read the letter in the Uptown H.S. *Newsletter* and it didn't say they should stop protesting. Nevertheless, clearly Annie read Maria Landon's position to mean that.

since this school is so into getting us to think for ourselves and everything, they'd want us to protest. But no.[11]

Although individual resistance has the potential to spark organized resistance that can lead to winning formal power, this occurs only under the rarest conditions. It is at least as likely, particularly when people begin to experience a sense of resignation in the face of continued existence of the rules, that resistance will erode or become coopted. In the video, Amy might be seen as someone who exemplifies this process. Although she resists the hat rule by wearing her hat, she has apparently already internalized the official rationale for the rule. Her position could have come right out of Jean Summers' mouth: "guys shouldn't wear hats. It's like a general rule. . . . If you're going to be in a working environment, you have to learn how to follow rules and regulations." Amy's resistance is just a step away from desistance.

The implications of forcing students into positions of individual resistance to a school rule are of much greater consequence than whether students ultimately wear hats in school or not. The real significance of the issue is that when students are forced into personal resistance, it reinforces in them a cynicism about public democratic activity.

Because UHS students have no formal institutional power, they must organize demonstrations, petitions, and other actions to try to influence school policy on a given issue. If such public organizing efforts fail, students retreat to exercise their private "democratic" rights of personal dress, individual resistance, and private study. This experience tells students that public action is futile: Don't bother. Private action is the answer. Withdraw from public life. Just resist. Wear your hat. Maybe cut out for lunch. Exercise your personal freedom. But leave the public world and the power structure intact. This part of the UHS student experience falls comfortably into line with the hegemonic American ideology of privatized citizenship.

Such an experience is especially problematic in a school whose philosophy and rhetoric call for developing public democratic values and attributes in young people. For at the same time that stu-

---

11. Field notes, 18 April 1991.

dents have obviously comprehended and internalized some of the school's democratic ideas and rhetoric, their day-to-day experience was one of a lack of power to affect the rules that governed their lives in school. The contradiction was not lost on the students.

Students' awareness of the contradiction could be heard in the words of Gail, Monica, and Annie. They all felt that the school should be held to a higher standard than other schools, just as it expects more of them than other schools expect of their students. For Gail, Uptown H.S. "is supposed to be such an alternative place and everything." Monica notes that "they want us to protest and all." For Annie, the school is "so into getting us to think for ourselves and everything." All three of these students perceived that Uptown H.S.'s agenda had something to do with getting them to be thoughtful social and political actors. In this sense the school's democratic intentions were being upheld. However, U.H.S. students' perceived lack of influence on issues that affected their daily lives, such as the schoolwide no hat rule and the no-outside-lunch rule for the Middle Section, was seen as especially contradictory.

I do not mean to detract from the many accomplishments of Uptown H.S., nor to minimize the strides it has taken to encourage students to become critical thinkers, and to develop public democratic values and capacities. As I have already documented, many aspects of the school's organization, structure, curriculum, and teaching contribute powerfully to students' development as public democratic citizens. Moreover, most of the students I spoke with informally seemed to hold positive views of the school, overall.

Nevertheless, I call attention to the lack of organized, school-sanctioned student participation in governance for two reasons. First, the lack of a student voice in school governance can begin to erode students' sense of ownership of their school. This can lead potentially to resentment of school authority, the formation of oppositional student cultures, and the eventual disengagement or resistance of students to the official school agenda. Second, excluding students from school governance means missing an obvious opportunity to develop students' capacities for public democratic participation. It means forfeiting a chance for students to develop, through personal experience, their understanding of democratic processes and their capacities for democratic participation.

Student Control/Ownership at Metropolitan H.S.

Students' perceived lack of ownership or control over certain aspects of school life at Uptown H.S. contrasts sharply with the perception of students at Metropolitan H.S. This was apparent in informal observations and conversations with students, as well as in student comments during a series of focus group meetings at Metropolitan H.S.

The most extensive discussion I had with MHS students about their perceived sense of control over school life came in the third focus group. The following is a rather telling, extended excerpt from the focus group discussion transcript.

> *DS*: What I'm thinking about is the question of control. . . . To what extent . . . do you feel you have any kind of input or control over how this school is run? Like [control] over the kinds of work that you do, or the classes or the homework, or the topics that you choose, or even about the way the school is set up and run, or how you're supposed to behave, any of those things. Do you feel like you have any input . . . ?
>
> [Several students]: Yeah. Yeah. Yes.
>
> *Freddy* [Latino male]: I think the school pretty much, we, the students have like a lot more input than they would have in any [other] school, where they would have no input, first of all. I mean we have an advisory group here that meets, like where different students meet in their advisory, and they take what they want to the Student Committee, and then the teachers' committee. So it's like a very democratic process that everything is run in this school. I think if more people got involved, and really cared, we'd have, the students would have even more control than they do now. Like we have a lot. We do have tremendous control.
>
> *DS*: So wait, how does it work again? It works through the advisories?
>
> [Several Students]: Yeah. Through the advisories—
>
> *Carlos* [Latino male]: Little groups of like eight students, they meet with a teacher. And they bring up a topic, or if there's

something you have a complaint about. Then a member of that group takes it to Student Committee—like there's one student for each advisory goes to the student committee, and brings up the issue. And Michael [one of the school co-directors] is there. And Michael is . . . always quiet. It's like just us talking. And mostly I don't talk, but, you know we discuss it, and we see what's up. . . . For example, some girls complained about girls smoking in the girls' bathroom. It took two or three complaints or something like that, and now they're going to set up a smoke alarm and everything. So, this is the process. You know anything can be done . . . except maybe a pinball machine in the bathroom, or something. You know, what is necessary for the school. . . .

DS: So are there regular meetings with Michael, like this?

Carlos: Once a week. And he has a staff meeting, which I think sometimes students are allowed to sit in.

Larry [African-American male]: Students are allowed to sit in if the teachers aren't talking *about* [individual] students. . . .

Freddy: Yeah. There's a meeting today that students will be able to sit in on, today at 3.

Carlos: And you have as much power as [any of the teachers]. You can raise up your hand and talk what you want, and complain or discuss, or whatever. It's not like, you know, the teacher, back in high school, back in Humanities, where you know . . .

Freddy: Yeah, everybody gets equal.

Ali [African-American female]: Um, also it's not even just like the student committees or whatever. Let's say you might not be on student committee. You can always go up to Michael or one of the teachers and say your complaint or whatever.

And . . . the teachers here really care about you. . . . And one thing they're never gonna do is attack you, personally. Maybe your ideas, you know, like in classes and stuff.

But here, this school is very unique, because here students definitely get a lot of control. A lot of control. . . . Like at other schools, forget it. What you say is not important. You're just a number on their computer and that's it. But here they treat you like real people. Because you are a real person, actually . . .

Everything here is really done for what's going to help you in your later life.

DS: Uh-huh. Anybody have any other points? . . . Larry, did you have any comment about any of that stuff, about control or feeling like you have any control?

Larry: . . . The latest thing is that the trip committee, one person from the trip committee went to the staff committee and they got the student trip sort of changed.

DS: Wait, what was it going to be? [Talking to the other students]: Did you guys hear about this, this student trip committee thing? Do you know about that?

[A few students speak up all together about it. Finally Carlos explains it.]

Carlos: It was [a choice between] an amusement park and the dude ranch, and the staff had already decided that we going to do the dude ranch. 'Cause the staff didn't like the rides. But the students wanted to go to the Amusement Park. And you know we said, "It's our trip. There are more students than teachers"—this and that. So . . . one of the students went to a staff meeting. And he got up all the votes from the students. And he went and the students won, over the staff.

DS: So they're going to go to the amusement park.

[Several students]: We're going to the amusement park.[12]

Regarding the issue of student ownership and control, the students here could hardly be any clearer. They not only have a general feeling of control and empowerment in the school, which is partially the result of the sense of belonging and safety that I discussed earlier. But they have an institutional power base in the school as well—the Student Committee.

Of course, many schools have student governments that do not necessarily translate into student power in the school. Sometimes

---

12. Focus Group #3 transcript, 7 May 1991.

student governments simply become instruments for coopting student leaders and winning student consent to school policies. Other times student governments become marginalized from the sentiments of the majority of students. But in the case of Metropolitan H.S., these students cited specific examples of the Student Committee having an impact on issues that really mattered to students.

From the outside, the issues cited may seem inconsequential. But dealing with a problem of smoking in the bathroom and reversing a staff decision regarding a school end-of-year trip represent concrete actions that helped improve student life at Metropolitan H.S. These kinds of experiences, taken in the context of the rest of the positive experiences students have of the school, go a long way toward building students' sense of self-respect and self-confidence as people who matter. To see this we need only look at Ali's precious statement: "But here they treat you like real people. Because you are a real person, actually."

Yes, Ali is a real person. And her realizing that she is a real person is one of the first steps toward becoming an independent social actor, who with the right preparation, could also become a public democratic political actor. An important part of the right preparation for public democratic citizenship is providing the opportunity for students to participate meaningfully in decisions that affect their day-to-day experience of school life. Metropolitan H.S. gives students that opportunity.

One African-American student in particular at Metropolitan H.S. left me with a strong sense of hope that carefully structured and skillfully run public high schools can make a difference in helping prepare students for public democratic citizenship. James, speaking in the first focus group, commented on how he felt the school had helped prepare him for the future, both as an individual and as a active member of the larger society.

James: I think that Metropolitan H.S. for me has done a number of things. And one of them is open my mind to the world and see that there's other places beyond Metro City. . . . And also I think that Metropolitan H.S. has made me aware of a lot of things that I wasn't aware of before. You know, social problems, political problems, as well as racial problems, and different things like that. And again, I think that it has put me in a position where I think that I will be able to succeed in higher education. . . .

I feel that I have a pretty good idea of where I want to be or where I'm going in later life. I'm in between where I want to go into a more corporate arena or you know, [make] some kind of change on the outside. Whether I'm inside the system or outside of the system I feel that I will try to make some change and make things better for the lower rung of people in the society.[13]

Many of the things James said seem to indicate that he has begun developing some of the values, attributes, and capacities that young people must possess if they are to become public democratic citizens, and through their efforts, help create a public democracy in the United States. His statement that he has become more aware of social and political problems suggests that he is beginning to develop a critical/analytical social outlook, examining social reality and identifying problems. His mention of racial problems points to an emerging critical social outlook as well, but also implies a concern for equality and justice. He speaks with an impressive self-confidence both about his preparation for college and about his sense of what he wants to do with his life and how he wants to contribute to society. His confidence in his own ability to have an impact on society as an independent social actor is one of the requisite qualities of public citizenship; that is, one is more likely to take public action if one feels that his/her actions will make a difference. James' specific interest in trying "to make some change and make things better for the lower rung of people in the society" highlights his appreciation of the importance of public life and his personal commitment to work for social change. It also demonstrates his belief in the equal right of everyone to the conditions necessary for their self-development. Finally, James' interest in helping the "lower rung of people in society" points to a budding commitment to an ethic of care and responsibility. James is a young man who will graduate high school with what he feels is an appropriate intellectual preparation for college, and what I believe is an essential foundation for public democratic citizenship.

---

13. Focus Group #1 transcript, 23 April 1991.

CHAPTER 9

In Search of Public Democratic Education

In Chapter 1 I highlighted several ominous trends in American social life, including an increasing concentration of control of the nation's wealth; the shrinking of the middle class and the growth of the lower class; a shifting of the country's tax burden from corporations and the wealthy to middle- and lower-income Americans; increasing homelessness; and the explosion of the American prison population into what *The Nation* has called "The American Gulag."[1] I argued that these unsettling developments were related to continuing patterns of mass alienation from government and democratic political processes. I argued throughout part I that our alienation from democratic processes was a logical outgrowth of our inheritance of a narrow, privatized vision of American democracy and democratic citizenship. Challenging the deterioration of American social life can only be accomplished by reinvigorating public life and working toward a more public vision and practice of democracy. Ordinary Americans must develop a more critical understanding of what is happening to their society, and who is benefitting from it. And they must step into the public sphere and begin to redirect their society toward the traditional goals of seeking equality, justice, and a democracy that serves the public, not just corporations and the wealthy.

---

1. Cover-page headline, *The Nation*, 20 February 1995.

This book calls on educators to make public high schools one of the central institutions in the struggle for public democracy. But beyond calling for public democratic education, this book develops and utilizes a tool for studying existing schools, which links what happens in schools to a clear theoretical understanding of what is meant by public democratic citizenship. In this way the book seeks to contribute to the development of a "language of possibility" of democratic educational theory,[2] as well as to a new "educational language of democratic imagery."[3]

The Importance of Public Democratic Education

America's dominant political tradition, that of privatized democratic ideas and practices, sanctifies the notion of self-serving individualism. It delegitimizes ideas of social connectedness that are the necessary foundation for collective action for the public good. The privatized democratic tradition contributes to a distrust, if not disgust, with all that is public. The result is Americans' overwhelming sense of alienation from public life.

Alienation seems especially marked among young Americans. In a focus group study conducted for People For the American Way, a social studies teacher summed up his students' attitudes toward involvement in community life in this way:

> My kids are going to look at [community involvement] and say, "Well, that's not going to buy me a Gucci shirt, or that's not going to buy me a pair of Fila tennis shoes or something. What's in it for me?"[4]

Robert Bellah and his co-authors uncover and analyze similar attitudes among Americans about their connections to communities, institutions and public life.[5] Such attitudes are often characterized

---

2. Aronowitz and Giroux, *Education under Siege*, 154.

3. Goodman, *Elementary Schooling for Critical Democracy*, 173.

4. People For the American Way, *Democracy's Next Generation: A Study of Youth and Teachers* (Washington, DC: People For the American Way, 1989), 57.

5. Robert N. Bellah, Richard Madsen, William M. Sullivan, Ann Swidler, and Steven M. Tipton, *Habits of the Heart* (Berkeley: University of California Press, 1985); Robert N. Bellah et al., *The Good Society* (New York: Alfred A. Knopf, 1991).

by "desire for private benefits at the expense of public provision."[6] These attitudes, which Bellah and his co-authors trace to "Lockean individualism," might be understood more simply as part of an ideology of irresponsible individualism. Irresponsible individualism contributes to, and helps justify, individual and collective inertia in the face of the decay of the nation's economic infrastructure; the deterioration of our cities; mounting social inequality; heightening bias-related conflict stemming from racism, sexism, and homophobia; and mushrooming violence throughout the nation. Irresponsible individualism exacerbates these centrifugal social forces, which threaten to tear our society apart.

In order to begin to confront the myriad social problems that the United States now faces, it is necessary to challenge dominant, privatized understandings of democracy and citizenship, and replace them with publicly oriented visions and practices of democratic citizenship. Such a "reinvigoration [of public life] is not an idealistic whim but the only realistic basis on which we can move ahead as a free people."[7]

The struggle for a new public democracy embraces both democratic ideology and political practice. Since education is a key institution for ideological and social reproduction, as well as resistance, schools can become sites in the struggle to define our future ideas and practices of democracy. When our educational system is allowed to contribute to reproducing ideologies of privatized democracy,

> schools produce spectators, not citizens. We are trained to watch and observe, to drop our franchise in a box, to support interest groups, and to seek private satisfaction while shunning the public world.[8]

But schools can become crucial institutions for helping young people begin to question and challenge privatistic notions of democracy. Progressive educators can gain control of their schools and remake them into sites of experience and learning which support public visions of democracy. To explore this possibility, this book set out to study two urban public alternative high schools that are attempting to create some form of democratic education for their students.

---

6. Bellah et al., *The Good Society*, 139.
7. Ibid., 141.
8. George H. Wood, *Schools That Work* (New York: Dutton, 1992), 80.

Studying Existing Schools

Schools do not exist in isolation from the larger society. The ways in which students experience school knowledge and make it their own (or not), are integrally linked with the social practices and ideas that are current in the society at large. Therefore in any study of "democratic" education, researchers must have a way of understanding their observations, which connects them to a particular tradition of democratic ideas. That is, in order to assess a school's democratic curriculum and practices, it is necessary to have in mind a clear idea of what one means by democracy and citizenship.

To this end, when I sought to examine the organization and practices of the two alternative high schools described in this book, it was necessary first to present a set of ideas that challenged dominant, privatized notions and practices of American democracy and citizenship. I have called this alternative vision of democracy *public democracy*.

Based on my synthesis of a number of political and social theorists' ideas, I developed an inventory of some of the values, attributes, and capacities that an ideal-typical public democratic citizen should possess. This set of citizenship characteristics included an ethic of care and responsibility; respect for the equal rights of all to the conditions necessary for their self-development; appreciation of the importance of the public; a critical/analytical social outlook; and a set of specific capacities necessary for public democratic participation.

Using these qualities of citizenship as goals toward which democratic schools ought to lead their students, I drew on the work of a number of leading education writers and practitioners to develop a vision of an ideal-typical democratic high school. This set of ideal principles for organizing and running a high school for public democracy then served as a tool for comparing and analyzing a few aspects of school life in Uptown and Metropolitan High Schools. Thus, I was able to tie my analysis of what I observed in the two schools to the tradition of American democratic ideas that I have called public democracy.

Reflections on Uptown and Metropolitan High Schools

Through their organization, curriculum, and teaching practices, Uptown and Metropolitan high schools do in fact appear to promote public democratic values, attributes and capacities in their students. By way of summary, I will comment on just a few examples which illustrate how these schools nurture public democratic citizenship.

Most importantly, these schools have created humane, caring, and safe environments, built around personal relationships that are consciously fostered among teachers, between teachers and students, and among students. By creating environments which encourage collaborative work among teachers and among students, and assigning teachers to take responsibility for the well-being of specific groups of students in advisory classes, the development of personal relationships becomes not only possible, but necessary. Anonymity and alienation are defeated. An ethic of care and responsibility is promoted. These schools model the possibility of community, which is the necessary foundation for public democratic life.

On the issue of encouraging students to respect the equal rights of all to the conditions necessary for their self-development, one critical aspect involves helping students come to terms with, and respect, cultural difference. In a multicultural society such as the United States, it is crucial for social stability that we all learn to understand and respect cultural diversity. The dangers of intolerance and conflict based on cultural difference can be seen from Bosnia and the newly independent states of the defunct Soviet Union, to Los Angeles and Crown Heights, Brooklyn.

Beyond the question of social stability, respect for cultural difference is also essential for public democracy. It is impossible to build a shared public life, in which people strive to create a common good, unless people have respect for cultural difference among their fellow citizens. There can be no ethic of care and responsibility, no sense of community, and thus no shared public life, where people view one another's differences with fear, mistrust, and hatred.

Both Uptown and Metropolitan High Schools encourage students to engage issues of cultural difference in a number of ways. At UHS, an obvious example can be found in the humanities curriculum themes studied in the school's Lower and Middle Sections. Yearlong investigations of such themes as "Justice: Comparative Systems of Law and Government," and "Non-European Traditions: Stability and Change in Selected Asian, Central American, and African States," provide students with multiple opportunities to wrestle with issues of cultural difference. Likewise at Metropolitan High School, in such classes as American history and "Sexist Society?," issues of diversity, equality, and justice are constant themes of readings and class discussions. Moreover, in both schools, the simple educational strategy of having students of different backgrounds do regular group research together, forces students to come to grips with each other's individual and cultural differences, within the natural context of working together to research and create common projects. Understanding and accepting difference is an essential step in coming to respect everyone's equal right to develop themselves in society.

Understanding and appreciating the importance of public life is another essential attribute of a public democratic citizen. When young people are encouraged to recognize the importance of public life, and their participation in it, the privatistic ideology of democracy is undermined. Both the video documentary class at Uptown H.S. and the action research class at Metropolitan H.S. demanded that students become engaged in public issues.

These two classes also encouraged students to take on a critical social outlook. Students in these classes were expected to investigate an issue through a variety of sources, question their own ideas, weigh the evidence gathered, and adopt a position on the issue. The position they took would then be expressed publicly either in writing a piece for publication or creating a video on the subject. Taking on a critical/analytical social outlook is a fundamental step toward public democratic citizenship.

There were a number of ways in which students in these two schools were encouraged to develop many of the specific capacities necessary for public democratic citizenship. Both schools put a heavy emphasis on students doing research, sometimes in collaborative teams, sometimes on their own. This is a critical citizenship skill which, once mastered, enables people to teach themselves whatever they need to know about new public issues, as they arise. Student research often involved interviewing people and thus analyzing spoken language; reading books and articles, and analyzing and producing written language; and in the case of the video class, looking at the language of images, and learning to express themselves in that medium. All these activities helped students develop their capacities to participate effectively in a public democracy.

The accomplishments of Uptown and Metropolitan High Schools provide signs of hope that urban high schools can help young people develop the values, attributes and capacities necessary for public democratic citizenship. Although, as in any school, not all students progressed as quickly or as far as some of their peers in mastering these citizenship capacities, most students I saw were engaged in the learning process. They were clearly on the road toward mastery of these citizenship skills.

However, creating public democratic high school education is by no means a simple or formulaic task. The people who created and taught in Uptown and Metropolitan High Schools found it necessary to design their schools in ways that were radically different from the design of traditional, comprehensive high schools. UHS and MHS were small, staff-run schools built around personal relationships among teachers and students, with curricula that emphasized research and the creation of knowledge by students.

The teachers in these schools were true professionals. They had powerful input into school decision-making on policy, direction, and programs. They worked together to design and constantly update their school's curriculum. They developed creative and flexible teaching approaches that allowed them to be educational "coaches." Rather than trying to transfer their knowledge to students, who would then regurgitate it on demand for periodic tests, these teachers guided and challenged students to discover and generate knowledge themselves, so they could take control of their own thinking and learning processes. At the same time, these teachers struggled to get students to look outward to understand events in the world—not only what happened, but what forces brought about these events, and who benefitted from them. They also encouraged students to see themselves as actors who could, with others, have an impact on events in their communities and in the world.

Meanwhile, the teachers at UHS and MHS, like all high school teachers, dealt with the complicated, ever-changing, often exasperating, ongoing challenge of helping meet adolescents' needs as they groped their way toward adulthood and citizenship. One important step toward adulthood and citizenship occurs when young people begin to develop their own individual and collective voices. Since school is the dominant public institution in high school students' lives, it is also the obvious place for them to express their developing public voices. Giving students opportunities to participate in decisions that affect their lives in school can provide critical lessons in public democratic citizenship.

But there is a potential dilemma here. While public democratic education calls for student voice and participation in some aspects of school decision-making, teachers also naturally want to *guide* students toward responsible, successful adulthood and citizenship. This sometimes means teaching young people to conform to certain adult expectations that may run counter to students' attempts to find and express their youthful voices.

The conflict over the no hat rule at UHS illustrated this dilemma. As has already been noted, in many ways the students at UHS were encouraged to develop their public democratic values, skills, and voices. But because of UHS students' perception that they had no voice in school decision making, particularly with regard to the no hat rule, many students simply resorted to individual, private resistance, in a guerrilla war of style against the rule. For these students, an ideology of privatized democracy was reinforced.

Prospects for Public Democratic Education

Examining Uptown and Metropolitan High Schools offers several insights into what is required to establish and sustain public democratic education in American high schools. As a number of recent books have pointed out, simply to make high school education more effective in developing students' intellectual abilities will require that schools be radically restructured in a number of ways consistent with the designs of the schools described here.[9]

First, schools should be built around relationships, between students and teachers, among teachers, and among students. This, in turn, will require that new schools be organized, and existing schools be reorganized, into much smaller functioning units than that of the traditional comprehensive high school. In addition, schools should establish advisory classes, or some other means of ensuring that teachers truly get to know students and vice versa.

---

9. A few examples are: Theodore R. Sizer, *Horace's Compromise*; George H. Wood, *Schools that Work*; Michelle Fine, *Framing Dropouts*.

Second, teaching and learning should be centered on students' work in research or inquiry learning projects and approaches. To facilitate these approaches, high school schedules will have to be redesigned, creating larger blocks of time and eliminating most forty minute periods. In addition, some breadth of curriculum "coverage" will have to be sacrificed so that greater depth of study might be obtained. This is the ideal encapsulated in the Coalition of Essential Schools' "less is more" principle.

Third, school administrators and teachers will have to embrace restructuring efforts. Administrators must not only allow, but actively encourage school restructuring, even when it means sacrificing some of their authority and giving greater autonomy to teachers. But even if school administrators favor change, real school restructuring cannot take place unless teachers also embrace school change. Teachers need to be willing to take on new responsibilities and give up some of the comfort of old routines, as they struggle to reconceptualize schooling, restructure their school days, and reinvent themselves as educators. Teachers will need to be supported in their own change processes, with extensive staff development that helps them rethink the goals and possibilities of education, and develop concrete new approaches to teaching.[10]

These are some of the basic prerequisites for changing American high schools to provide a better education to young people. However, more is required of educators who wish to establish and sustain *schools for public democracy*. First, these educators need to gain a clear understanding of what is meant by public democratic citizenship. It is not enough to say, as all American educators would, that they want to prepare students for citizenship. As I have argued in this book, the kind of citizenship for which most young Americans are trained is falling far short of protecting us from increasing levels of social injustice, inequality, violence, racism, crime, fear, social decay, and an overall meanness of spirit that has progressively

---

10. Reconceptualizing schooling requires, first, that teachers and administrators read about, analyze, critique, discuss, and debate big ideas, such as the purposes of education in a democratic society. These discussions must then connect the big ideas with practical concerns, such as how to accomplish the real purposes of education by altering what goes on in schools and in individual classrooms. Richard Gibboney has described one model of teacher/ administrator dialogue which places democratic, intellectual discussion at the center of the school reform process. See Gibboney, *The Stone Trumpet*, 205–21.

gripped the nation. Public democratic citizenship is the only clear democratic antidote to these dangerous social trends.

Once educators have a clear conception of public democratic citizenship, they will still need to develop a means for examining their school organization and practice, as well as any proposed changes, to see the extent to which they promote public democratic citizenship. It is my hope that the analytical tools developed in this book will provide a starting point for such undertakings.

The idea of building public democracy might seem idealistic, especially now, when a politics of anger, blame, retribution, selfishness, and limited possibilities has captured the national mood. But public democratic citizenship, which entails intelligent and effective participation by all citizens in shaping their society, may be the only creative, democratic exit from the cul-de-sac of contemporary politics.

Educators, whose role has always been to prepare young people to participate in society, must decide how we want them to participate, and in what kind of society. We can continue to educate students so that they will passively accept an increasingly dark and limited social future. Or we can strive to create education for public democracy.

If we choose public democracy, we can remake public education to prepare young people to build a new public life and begin to reshape American society into the kind of place we've always been told it could be: a place of tolerance, care, justice, individual and social responsibility, and equal opportunity for all our citizens to develop themselves fully and prosper. If we care about all our children, do we really have any choice?

Bibliography

Books

Apple, Michael. *Ideology and Curriculum.* New York: Routledge and Kegan Paul, 1979.

Aronowitz, Stanley and Henry Giroux. *Postmodern Education.* Minneapolis: University of Minnesota Press, 1991.

Aronowitz, Stanley and Henry Giroux. *Education under Siege.* London: Routledge and Kegan Paul, 1987.

Barber, Benjamin. *Strong Democracy.* Los Angeles: University of California Press, 1984.

Belenky, M. F., B. Clinchy, N. Goldberger, and J. Tarule. *Women's Ways of Knowing.* New York: Basic Books, 1986.

Bellah, Robert N., Richard Madsen, William M. Sullivan, Ann Swidler, and Steven M. Tipton. *The Good Society.* New York: Alfred A. Knopf, 1991.

Bellah, Robert N., Richard Madsen, William M. Sullivan, Ann Swidler, and Steven M. Tipton. *Habits of the Heart.* Berkeley: University of California Press, 1985.

Bentham, Jeremy. *A Bentham Reader.* Edited by Mary Peter Mack. New York: Pegasus, 1969.

Bigelow, Bill, L. Christensen, S. Karp, B. Miner, and B. Peterson, eds. *Rethinking Our Classrooms: Teaching for Equity and Justice.* Milwaukee, WI: Rethinking Schools Limited, 1994.

Boyer, Ernest L. *High School.* New York: Harper & Row, 1983.

Brouwer, Steve. *Sharing the Pie: A Disturbing Picture of the U.S. Economy.* Carlisle, PA: Big Picture Books, 1992.

Campbell, Bruce. *The American Electorate.* New York: Holt, Rhinehart, Winston, 1979.

Cohen, Joshua and Joel Rogers. *On Democracy: Toward a Transformation of American Society.* New York: Penguin Books, 1984.

Connell, R. W. *The Child's Construction of Politics.* Carlton, Australia: Melbourne University Press, 1971.

Connell, R. W., D. J. Ashenden, S. Kessler, and G. W. Dowsett. *Making the Difference.* Boston: George Allen and Unwin, 1982.

Dahl, Robert. *Democracy and Its Critics.* New Haven: Yale University Press, 1989.

Dewey, John. *Democracy and Education.* New York: The Free Press, 1966, orig. 1916.

———. *The Public and Its Problems.* Chicago: Swallow Press, 1988, orig. 1927.

Educators for Social Responsibility. *Making History: A Social Studies Curriculum in the Participation Series.* Cambridge, MA: Boston Area Educators for Social Responsibility, 1984.

Ewen, Stuart. *All Consuming Images.* New York: Basic Books, 1988.

Fine, Michelle. *Framing Dropouts.* Albany: SUNY Press, 1991.

Foxfire Fund. *Hands On: A Journal for Teachers.* Rabun Gap, GA: The Foxfire Fund, Inc.

Freedman, Samuel G. *Small Victories.* New York: Harper & Row, 1990.

Freire, Paulo. *Pedagogy of the Oppressed.* New York: Continuum, 1981.

Gardner, Howard. *Frames of Mind.* New York: Basic Books, 1983.

Gibboney, Richard A. *The Stone Trumpet.* Albany: SUNY Press, 1994.

Gilligan, Carol. *In a Different Voice.* Cambridge, MA: Harvard University Press, 1982.

Giroux, Henry. *Schooling and the Struggle for Public Life.* Minneapolis: University of Minnesota Press, 1988.

Goodman, Jesse. *Elementary Schooling for Critical Democracy.* Albany: SUNY Press, 1992.

Gould, Carol. *Rethinking Democracy: Freedom and Social Cooperation in Politics, Economy and Society*. New York: Cambridge University Press, 1988.

Gramsci, Antonio. *Selections from the Prison Notebooks*. Edited and translated by Quintin Hoare and Geoffrey Nowell. New York: International Publishers, 1985.

Greenberg, Edward S. *The American Political System: A Radical Approach*. Boston: Little, Brown and Co., 1983.

Greenstein, Fred. *Children and Politics*. New Haven: Yale University Press, 1965.

Hamilton, Alexander, John Jay, and James Madison. *The Federalist Papers*. Edited by Clinton Rossiter. New York: New American Library, 1961.

Hess, Robert and Judith Torney. *The Development of Political Attitudes in Children*. Garden City, NY: Doubleday, 1968.

Hobbes, Thomas. *Leviathan*. Edited by Michael Oakeshott. New York: Collier Books, 1962.

hooks, bell. *Talking Back: Thinking Feminist, Thinking Black*. Boston: South End Press, 1989.

Hyman, Herbert. *Political Socialization*. Glencoe: The Free Press, 1959.

Jaggar, Alison and Paula Rothenberg, eds. *Feminist Frameworks*. New York: McGraw-Hill, 1984.

Jefferson, Thomas. *Notes on the State of Virginia*. Edited by William Peden. New York: W. W. Norton and Co., 1982, orig. 1787.

————. *Crusade against Ignorance: Thomas Jefferson on Education*. Edited by Gordon C. Lee. New York: Teachers College Press, 1966.

Krueger, Richard A. *Focus Groups: A Practical Guide for Applied Research*. Newbury Park, CA: Sage Publications, 1988.

Lappe, Francis Moore. *Rediscovering America's Values*. New York: Ballantine Books, 1989.

Lukacs, Georg. *History and Class Consciousness*. Cambridge, MA: MIT Press, 1971.

MacPherson, C. B. *The Political Theory of Possessive Individualism*. London: Oxford University Press, 1962.

Mannheim, Karl. *Ideology and Utopia*. New York: Harcourt Brace Jovanovich, 1936.

Marable, Manning. *The Crisis of Color and Democracy*. Monroe, ME: Common Courage Press, 1992.

Marx, Karl and Frederick Engels. *The Communist Manifesto*. New York: Pocket Books, 1964.

———. *The German Ideology*. New York: International Publishers, 1970.

McLaren, Peter. *Life in Schools*. New York: Longman, 1989.

Mill, John Stuart. *Representative Government*. Edited by Currin V. Shields. New York: Bobbs-Merrill, 1958.

———. *Utilitarianism, with Critical Essays*. Edited by Samuel Gorovitz. New York: Bobbs-Merrill, 1971.

Mills, C. Wright. *Power, Politics and People*. Edited by Irving Louis Horowitz. New York: Oxford University Press, 1963.

———. *The Sociological Imagination*. New York: Oxford University Press, 1959.

Morgan, David L. *Focus Groups as Qualitative Research* Newbury Park, CA: Sage Publications, 1988.

Newmann, Fred, ed. *Student Engagement and Achievement in American Secondary Schools*. New York: Teachers College Press, 1992.

Pateman, Carole. *The Problem of Political Obligation: A Critique of Liberal Theory*. Berkeley: University of California Press, 1985.

People For the American Way. *Democracy's Next Generation. A Study of Youth and Teachers*. Washington, DC: People For the American Way, 1989.

Perrone, Vito. *A Letter to Teachers*. San Francisco: Josey-Bass Publishers, 1991.

Phillips, Kevin. *The Politics of Rich and Poor*. New York: Random House, 1990.

———. *Boiling Point: Democrats, Republicans and the Decline of Middle-Class Prosperity*. New York: Harper Collins, 1994, 279.

Piaget, Jean. *The Development of Thought: Equilibration of Cognitive Structures*. New York: Viking Press, 1977.

Piven, Frances Fox and Richard A. Cloward. *Why Americans Don't Vote*. New York: Pantheon Books, 1988.

Plamenatz, John. *The English Utilitarians*. Oxford: Basil Blackwell and Mott, 1966.

Rose, Mike. *Lives on the Boundary*. New York: Penguin Books, 1990.

Rousseau, Jean-Jacques. *The Social Contract*. New York: Penguin Books, 1985, orig. 1762.

Russell, Bertrand. *A History of Western Philosophy*. New York: Touchstone Books, 1982.

Schattschneider, E. E. *The Semi-Sovereign People*. Hinsdale, IL: Dryden Press, 1975, orig. 1960.

Schumpeter, Joseph. *Capitalism, Socialism and Democracy*. New York: Harper Torchbooks, 1950, orig. 1942.

Shapiro, Andrew L. *We're Number One!* New York: Vintage Books, 1992.

Shor, Ira. *Critical Teaching and Everyday Life*. Boston: South End Press, 1980.

———. *Empowering Education*. Chicago: University of Chicago Press, 1992.

Silvert, Kalman. *The Reason for Democracy*. New York: Viking Press, 1976.

Sizer, Theodore. *Horace's Compromise*. Boston: Houghton Mifflin, 1984.

———. *Horace's School*. Boston: Houghton Mifflin, 1992.

Somerville, John and Ronald E. Santoni, eds. *Social and Political Philosophy*. Garden City, NY: Anchor Books, Doubleday and Co., 1963.

Southern Poverty Law Center. *The Shadow of Hate: A History of Intolerance in America* (video and teaching materials). Montgomery, Alabama: Southern Poverty Law Center, Teaching Tolerance project, 1995.

Takaki, Ronald. *A Different Mirror: A History of Multicultural America*. New York: Little, Brown, 1993.

Truman, David B. *The Governmental Process: Political Interests and Public Opinion*. New York: Alfred A. Knopf, 1951.

Weber, Max. *Economy and Society*. Edited by Guenther Roth and Claus Wittich. Berkeley: University of California Press, 1968.

Weiler, Kathleen. *Women Teaching for Change*. South Hadley, MA: Bergin and Garvey, 1988.

Wentworth, William. *Context and Understanding*. New York: Elsevier, 1980.

Williams, Raymond. *Marxism and Literature*. New York: Oxford University Press, 1977.

Willis, Paul. *Learning to Labor*. New York: Columbia University Press, 1981.

Wilson, William J. *The Declining Significance of Race: Blacks and Changing American Institutions*. Chicago: University of Chicago Press, 1978.

Wood, George H. *Schools That Work*. New York: Dutton, 1992.

Articles and Essays

Althusser, Louis. "Ideology and Ideological State Apparatuses Notes Towards an Investigation." In *Lenin and Philosophy and Other Essays*. New York: Monthly Review Press, 1971.

Aronowitz, Stanley. "A Different Perspective on Educational Inequality." In *Experiencing Diversity: Toward Educational Equity*, ed. Frank Pignatelli and Susanna W. Pflaum, 25–46. Thousand Oaks, CA: Corwin Press, 1994.

———. "The Future of Socialism?" *Social Text* 24 (1990): 85–116.

Berke, Richard. "Experts Say Low 1988 Turnout May Be Repeated." *New York Times*, 13 November 1988.

Boyte, Harry C. "Turning On Youth to Politics." *The Nation* 252 (13 May 1991).

Brenner, Johanna. "Feminist Political Discourses: Radical versus Liberal Approaches to the Feminization of Poverty and Comparable Worth." In *Women, Class and the Feminist Imagination*, ed. Karen V. Hansen and Ilene J. Philipson, 494. Philadelphia: Temple University Press, 1990.

Burns, J. "Utilitarianism and Democracy." In J. S. Mill, *Utilitarianism with Critical Essays*, ed. Samuel Gorovitz, 270. New York: Bobbs-Merrill Co., 1971.

Carpignano, Paolo, Robin Andersen, Stanley Aronowitz, and William DiFazio. "Chatter in the Age of Electronic Reproduction: Talk Television and the 'Public Mind,' " *Social Text* 25/26 (1990).

Christensen, Linda. "Unlearning the Myths that Bind Us." In *Rethinking Our Classrooms: Teaching for Equity and Justice*, ed. Bill Bigelow, L. Christensen, S. Karp, B. Miner, and B. Peterson, 8–13. Milwaukee, WI: Rethinking Schools Limited, 1994.

Cowell, Alan. "Pope Challenges Brazil Leaders on Behalf of Poor." *New York Times* 15 October 1991, A15.

Cummins, Jim. "Empowering Minority Students: A Framework for Intervention." *Harvard Education Review* 56 (February 1986): 23.

Dietz, Mary. "Context Is All: Feminism and Theories of Citizenship." *Daedalus* 116.4 (Fall 1987): 1–24.

Ehrenreich, Barbara. "Life Without Father: Reconsidering Socialist-Feminist Theory." In *Women, Class and the Feminist Imagination*, ed. Karen V. Hansen and Ilene J. Philipson, 268–76. Philadelphia: Temple University Press, 1990.

Eisenstein, Zillah. "Constructing a Theory of Capitalist patriarchy and Socialist Feminism." In *Women, Class and the Feminist Imagination*, ed. Karen V. Hansen and Ilene J. Philipson, 268–76. Philadelphia: Temple University Press, 1990.

Ewen, Stuart and Elizabeth Ewen. "Images of Democracy." In *Channels of Desire: Mass Images and the Shaping of American Consciousness*, 169–82. New York: McGraw-Hill, 1982.

Fraser, Nancy. "Rethinking the Public Sphere: A Contribution to the Critique of Actually Existing Democracy." *Social Text* 25/26 (1990).

Goleman, Daniel. "Psychologists Find Ways to Break Racism's Hold." *New York Times*, 5 September 1989, C1.

Gould, Carol C. "Private Rights and Public Virtues: Women, the Family and Democracy." In *Beyond Domination: New Perspectives on Women and Philosophy*, ed. Carol C. Gould, 5. Totowa, NJ: Rowman and Allanheld, 1984.

Grannis, Joseph C. "The School as a Model of Society." In *The Learning of Political Behavior*, ed. Norman Adler and Charles Harrington. Glenview, IL: Scott, Foresman and Co., 1970.

Gross, Mara. "Reflection in Action: A Practitioner's Study of Four High School Students' Experience in Community Service." Ed.D. diss., Teachers College, Columbia University, 1991.

Heath, Shirley Brice. "Questioning at Home and at School: A Comparative Study." In *Doing the Ethnography of Schooling*, ed. George Spindler. New York: Holt, Rinehart and Winston, 1982.

Jefferson, Thomas. "Letter to John Taylor." In *Social and Political Philosophy*, ed. John Somerville and Ronald Santoni, 252–54. Garden City, NY: Anchor Books, 1963.

————. "Letter to Isaac A. Tiffany." In *Social and Political Philosophy*, ed. John Somerville and Ronald Santoni, 280. Garden City, NY: Anchor Books, 1963.

Karp, Walter. "The Two Americas." In *Buried Alive: Essays on Our Endangered Republic*, New York: Franklin Square Press, 1992.

Locke, John. "An Essay Concerning the True Original Extent and End of Civil Government." Excerpted in *Social and Political Philosophy*, ed. John Somerville and Ronald E. Santoni, 169–204. Garden City, NY: Anchor Books, Doubleday and Co., 1963.

"Low-Income Voters' Turnout Fell in 1994, Census Reports." *New York Times*, 11 June 1995, 28.

Mansbridge, Jane. "Feminism and Democracy." *The American Prospect* 1 (Spring 1990): 127. Quoted in Nancy Fraser. "Rethinking the Public Sphere: A Contribution to the Critique of Actually Existing Democracy," *Social Text* 25/26 (1990).

"Middle Class Shrinks, U.S. Says." *New York Times*, 22 February 1992, I9.

Nasar, Sylvia. "The Rich Get Richer, But Never the Same Way Twice." *The New York Times*, 16 August 1992: section 4, 3.

Newmann, Fred. "Student Engagement in Academic Work: Expanding the Perspective on Secondary School Effectiveness." In *Rethinking Effective Schools*, ed. J. Bliss and W. Firestone. Englewood Cliffs, NJ: Prentice Hall, 1991.

Newmann, Fred, G. Wehlage, and S. Lamborn. "Significance and Sources of Student Engagement." In *Student Engagement and Achievement in American Secondary Schools*, ed. F. Newmann. New York: Teachers College Press, 1992.

Ogbu, John. "Ethnoecology of Urban Schooling." In *Cities of the United States*, ed. Leith Mullings. New York: Columbia University Press, 1987.

Oreskes, Michael. "A Trait of Today's Youth: Apathy to Public Affairs." *The New York Times*, 28 June 1990.

————. "Alienation from Government Grows, Poll Finds," *New York Times*, 19 September 1990.

Palonsky, Stuart. "Political Socialization in Elementary Schools." *The Elementary School Journal* 87.5 (1987).

Pear, Robert. "55% Voting Rate Reverses 30-Year Decline." *New York Times*, 5 November 1992.

Sack, Kevin. "Andrew Cuomo." *The New York Times Magazine*, 27 March 1994, 42.

Shannon, Patrick. "Developing Democratic Voices." *The Reading Teacher*, 47.2, (October 1993).

Tronto, Joan. "Beyond Gender Difference to a Theory of Care." *Signs* 12.4, (1987).

West, Cornel. "Learning to Talk of Race." *The New York Times Magazine*, 2 August 1992.

Wicker, Tom. "The Iron Medal." *The New York Times*, 7 January 1991.

Wilcox, Kathleen. "Differential Socialization in the Classroom: Implications for Equal Opportunity." In *Doing the Ethnography of Schooling*, ed. George Spindler. New York: Holt, Rinehart and Winston, 1982.

Index

Alienation, political, 12–13; as a factor in domination, 17
Alternative high schools, in Metro City, 111
Althusser, Louis, 22, 25, 28

Barber, Benjamin, 103
Bellah, Robert, 172
Bentham, Jeremy, 44, 45
Bill of Rights, 32
Brenner, Johanna, 73

Chavez, Cesar, 23
Citizenship: as artificial patriotism, 13; consequences of crisis of, 13–17; crisis of, 12. *See also* Public democratic citizenship; School practices, for public democratic citizenship
Cloward, Richard A., 52–54
Cohen, Joshua, 55
Coalition of Essential Schools (CES), some guiding principles, 114, 179
Connell, R. W., 85
Constitution, U.S., 32, 33
Counterpublics, 65, 75–77, 92; as challenge to privatized democracy,

65, 75–77; education through, 76; influenced by ideology of privatized democracy, 76; need for communication among, 77; need for ethic of care and responsibility, 77

Dahl, Robert, 47
Democracy: as slogan, 49–50; Cold War rhetoric and, 51; competing understandings of, 3–4, 29, 31; consumer, as substitute for political, 50–51; direct, founders' antipathy toward, 32; hegemonic ideology of, 18, 26, 28; public education and expansion of, 27–29, 107–108; social activist groups and expansion of, 27. *See also* Privatized democracy; Public democracy
Democratic urban education, need for research on, 84
Dewey, John, 4, 5, 29; corporate undermining of the public sphere, 59; education for public democracy, 2, 62–63; need for public discussion of issues, 58;

Dewey, John (*continued*)
    need for social inquiry and
    inquiry education, 62–63;
    utilitarianism, 46
Diversity, respecting cultural and
    racial, 79, 80, 93–94, 175–76

Education: and language of democratic
    imagery, 2–3; and language of
    possibility, 2; purposes of, 1–2;
    role preparing young people for
    citizenship, 28. *See also* Schools;
    School practices, for public
    democratic citizenship
Engagement in school programs
    characteristics of schools which
        contribute to, 87–89
    intrinsic interest, real-world
        meaning, and student
        ownership: at UHS, 137–39; at
        MHS, 142–43, 166–69
    membership and safety in school
        community, 117–127: caring
        relationships, 118, 119; school
        size and house system, 118–
        119; advisory systems, 119–
        121; class size, 121–122;
        physical space, 122–124; safety,
        physical and emotional, 124–
        127
    need for engagement, 87
Equality and social justice, 92–94, 176
Ethic of care and responsibility, 5,
    66–68; key public democratic
    citizenship value, 79, 80; need for
    counterpublics to adopt this ethic,
    77; promoting this ethic at MHS
    and UHS, 127–128, 175

Family values discourse, 69–70
Federalist Papers, The, 4, 11, 29;
    constitution's protection of
    property and liberty, 33; ideas
    contributing to conceptions of
    privatized democracy, 42
Federalism, 33

Feminism, as counterpublic, 65;
    contributions to public democracy,
    66–75; equality, 66, 72–74;
    interdependence of individuals,
    66; private concerns to public
    issues, 68–72. *See also* Ethic of
    care and responsibility
Fine, Michelle, 84, 119
Fraser, Nancy, 5, 29; control of public
    discussion by dominant groups,
    73; counterpublics, 65; public
    nature of private issues, 70–71
Freire, Paulo, 99
Funding levels, Metro City alternative
    high schools, 121–122

Gilligan, Carol, 5, 29, 67
Gould, Carol, 5, 29; conditions for
    self-development, access to, 73;
    freedom as self-development, 68;
    relationship between individuals
    and community, 68
Goodman, Jesse, 2–3
Gramsci, Antonio, 20, 27–28
Grannis, Joseph, 103

Hamilton, Alexander, 4, 33
Hegemony: alternative, 19; briefly
    explained, 4, 17, 18–19; estab-
    lishing a new democratic, 28
Hobbes, Thomas, 4, 29
Homelessness, 15–16

Ideological change, need for, 77–78
Ideology: and social change, 24–25;
    and social stability, 25, 26
Inequality, 25, 28; consumer
    democracy's disguising of, 50;
    economic, leading to political
    inequality, 14–15, 35–36, 38,
    40–42, 48–49; pluralism's
    acceptance of, 48; of women and
    other subordinate groups, 72
Intellectuals: need for all to devlop as,
    20, 24, 63; organic, 23, 24–26,
    28; role in building public

democracy, 20, 26; role in challenging existing social order, 20; role in establishing and maintaining hegemony, 19–20; traditional, 20–24

Jay, John, 4, 33
Jefferson, Thomas, 4, 5, 29; education for democracy, 1–2, 34–36, 83; views compared with Rousseau's, 38–41; views on popular participation contrasted with Madison's, 34–39, 42; views shared with Madison's, 33–34
Justice, social, and equality, 92–94

King, Martin Luther, Jr., 23

Liberalism, as origin of American democratic ideologies, 31
Locke, John, 4, 5, 29, 32
Lower class, growing, 14–15

MacPherson, C. B., ideology of possessive individualism, 32
Madison, James, 4, 5, 33; views on popular participation compared to Jefferson's and Rousseau's, 34–42
Marabel, Manning, 63–65
McKinley, William, 52
Metropolitan High School (MHS): action research class, 145–50; background, 114–115; citizenship education in, 116, 169–70; community service, 141–42; curriculum and teaching, 139–42; goals, 115–116; inquiry learning in, 115, 140–41; scheduling, 141
Middle class, shrinking, 14–15
Mill, James, 44, 45
Mill, John Stuart, 44; buffering against popular influence on government, 45; primacy of personal freedom and individualism, 45
Mills, C. Wright, 4, 5, 29; Americans as "altogether private" people, 62;

citizens' lack of influence in public affairs, 59; linking education with social movements, 63; need for public discussion of issues, 58; need for education for public democracy, 63; personal concerns to social issues, 63, 71
Multicultural democracy, 63–64, 65

Oreskes, Michael, 12

Pateman, Carole, 29, 72n
People for the American Way, 172
Persian Gulf War, 61
Piven, Frances Fox, 52–54
Pluralism, 29, 47–50; basic assumptions, 47; claim that citizens cannot be self-governing, 48; connection to utilitarianism, 47; as ideological limit on participation, 49; inequality in, 48; public life as spectacle, 49
Political participation
  dominant conceptions of democracy and, 11, 17–18
  capitalist political economy and limits on, 54–55
  public democracy and, 57
  traditional practice of democracy and, 18
  voting limits and, 52–56: for low-income whites, 52–53; for blacks, 53; for women, 53
Political socialization, in schools, 85
Prisons, 15, 171
Privatized democracy, 4–5, 29; capitalist political economy and, 54–55; ideological roots of, 31–34, 38, 39, 42; limits on voting and, 52–54; Nineteenth- and Twentieth-Century theoretical contributions to, 43–51
Public democracy, 4–5, 29
  ideological roots of, 34–42
  need for, 17–18, 107

Public democracy (*continued*)
  Twentieth-Century theoretical
    contributions to: Brenner, 73;
    Dewey and Mills, 57–64, 71;
    Gilligan, 67; Gould, 68, 73;
    feminism, 66–75; Fraser, 65,
    70–71, 73; Marabel, 63–64, 65
Public democratic citizenship:
    characteristics of, 78–81;
    nurturing at MHS and UHS,
    175–76. *See also* School practices,
    for public democratic citizenship
Public democratic education, 62–64,
    84, 89–105; importance of, 172–73
Public spheres: citizens as passive
    listeners and viewers of, 60;
    domination by corporate interests,
    59; lack of equal participation in,
    73–74; problems due to mass
    media, 60; private vs. public,
    68–72

Research, qualitative, 3, 85–86;
    methods used in this study,
    108–109
Resistance: to dominant ideologies and
    social practices, 61–62; to
    socialization, 25–26
Rights, individual: of appropriation,
    32; protection of, 11, 31–32
Rogers, Joel, 55
Rose, Mike, 97
Rousseau, Jean-Jacques, 4, 5, 29;
    views on popular participation
    compared to Jefferson's and
    Madison's, 34–42

Schattschneider, E. E., 47
Schools: importance of personal
    relationships in, 119, 177,
    178, recommendations for
    restructuring, 178–80; roles in
    developing democratic publics,
    63–64; sites for ideological
    contestation and social change,

25, 29; sites for ideological and
    social reproduction, 25
School practices, for public democratic
    citizenship, 90–105
  critical examination of social reality,
    96–97
  discussing and acting on public
    issues, 95–96
  developing students' capacities for
    public democratic participation,
    97–105; active listening and
    collaboration, 98–100; critical
    analysis and self-expression,
    97–98; knowledge of rights and
    government processes, 98;
    modeling democratic participation,
    103–105; self-directed learning,
    102; understanding complexities
    and connections of issues, 100;
    understanding social construction
    of knowledge, 101–102
  exploring theme of interdependence,
    90–92
  study of equality and social justice,
    92–94
  study of cultural diversity, 93–96
Schumpeter, Joseph, 47
Social movements: as counterpublics,
    64–65; education and, 62–64;
    study of, 93
Smith, Adam, 29

Tax burden, 15
Times Mirror Center for the People
    and the Press, 12
Truman, David, 47

Uptown High School (UHS)
    background, 112–13
  curriculum and teaching, Lower
    and Middle Section 129–35:
    assessment and family confer-
    ences, 134–135; community
    service, 133–134; humanities/

social studies, 130–131; math/
science, 131–133; scheduling, 130
curriculum and teaching, Upper
Section, 135–137; graduation
committee, 135; organizing
components of, 135–136;
portfolios, 137
goal of citizenship education, 113
guiding principles, 114
habits of mind, 113
lack of channels for student input
on school rules, 163, 165
no hats rule, 158–159, 161–162
no hats video, 160–161

resistance, limits of, 164
video documentary class, 151–158
Urban crisis, 16; in schools, 84
Utilitarianism, 29, 43–49; basic
assumptions of, 44; connection to
laissez-faire economic theory, 46,
49; connection to federalism, 49;
devalutaion of public life and
government, 46, 49

Wealth, concentration of, 14
Wentworth, William, 85
Williams, Raymond, 19
Willis, Paul, 25